C0-DVV-081

Foundation and Pillars
of the Christian Faith

Compiled by Maurice Hoppe

Illustrations by John Fraser

TEACH Services, Inc.
P U B L I S H I N G
www.TEACHServices.com • (800) 367-1844

World rights reserved. This book or any portion thereof may not be copied or reproduced in any form or manner whatever, except as provided by law, without the written permission of the publisher, except by a reviewer who may quote brief passages in a review.

The author assumes full responsibility for the accuracy of all facts and quotations as cited in this book. The opinions expressed in this book are the author's personal views and interpretations, and do not necessarily reflect those of the publisher.

This book is provided with the understanding that the publisher is not engaged in giving spiritual, legal, medical, or other professional advice. If authoritative advice is needed, the reader should seek the counsel of a competent professional.

Copyright © 2015 TEACH Services, Inc.
ISBN-13: 978-1-4796-0505-7 (Paperback)
ISBN-13: 978-1-4796-0506-4 (ePub)
ISBN-13: 978-1-4796-0507-1 (Mobi)
Library of Congress Control Number: 2015909067

All scripture quotations, unless otherwise noted, are taken from the New King James Version®. Copyright © 1982 by Thomas Nelson, Inc. Used by permission. All rights reserved.

Scripture quotations marked NASB are taken from the New American Standard Bible®, Copyright © 1960, 1962, 1968, 1971, 1972, 1973, 1975, 1977, 1995 by The Lockman Foundation. Used by permission.

Scripture quotations marked NIV are taken from the Holy Bible, New International Version®, NIV®. Copyright © 1973, 1978, 1984, 2011 by Biblica, Inc.™ Used by permission of Zondervan. All rights reserved worldwide.

Scripture quotations marked RSV are taken from the Revised Standard Version of the Bible, copyright 1952 [2nd edition, 1971] by the Division of Christian Education of the National Council of the Churches of Christ in the United States of America. Used by permission. All rights reserved.

Published by

TEACH Services, Inc.
PUBLISHING
www.TEACHServices.com • (800) 367-1844

Table of Contents

Introduction

This book—*Foundation and Pillars of the Christian Faith*—is designed to be used as a study guide rather than a book to be read and laid aside. Vital information is contained in its pages.

Italicized words in Bible texts indicate that the words or phrases do not appear in the original manuscripts but were added some time later by a copyist.

Bible texts referenced in the Spirit of Prophecy quotations are quoted in full prior to the references.

"Many have come to deny doctrines which are the very pillars of the Christian faith. The great *facts of creation* as presented by the inspired writers, the *fall of man,* the *atonement,* and the *perpetuity of the law of God,* are practically rejected, either wholly or in part, by a large share of the professedly Christian world" (*The Great Controversy,* p. 583, emphasis added).

"The passing of the time in 1844 was a period of great events, opening to our astonished eyes the *cleansing of the sanctuary* transpiring in heaven, and having decided relation to God's people upon the earth, [also] the *first and second angels' messages and the third,* unfurling the banner on which was inscribed, 'The commandments of God and the faith of Jesus.' One of the landmarks under this message was the temple of God, seen by His truth-loving people in heaven, and the ark containing the *law of God.* The light of the Sabbath of the fourth commandment flashed its strong rays in the pathway of the transgressors of God's law. The *nonimmortality of the wicked* is an old landmark. I can call to mind nothing more that can come under the head of the old landmarks" (*Counsels to Writers and Editors,* pp. 30, 31, emphasis added).

Preface
A Treatise from Inspiration

"Your word *is* a lamp to my feet and a light to my path." Psalm 119:105.

Inspiration reveals to us, at the very beginning of the Bible, the entrance of sin into this world, and the consequences for this sin—eternal death (see Genesis 2:17; Romans 6:23; Ezekiel 33:11). It also tells us of the mercy, compassion, and yearning of the Creator for the restoration of His creatures. As we study God's Word, we recognize more and more the dire consequences of sin and its results, the utter hopelessness of man, in himself, to escape this doom. And through inspiration we are led to understand more fully this mercy, compassion, and yearning of the Creator for man's salvation. We then can see clearly that this theme, man's restoration into the image of God, is the very central theme of the Bible. It is the consuming topic, the all-encompassing message that God wants us to understand. Then the following words become not only understandable but logical and, in fact, compelling.

"The central theme of the Bible, the theme about which every other in the whole book clusters, is the redemption plan, the restoration in the human soul of the image of God. From the first intimation of hope in the sentence pronounced in Eden to that last glorious promise of the Revelation, 'They shall see His face; and His name shall be in their foreheads' (Revelation 22:4), the burden of every book and every passage of the Bible is the unfolding of this wondrous theme,—man's uplifting,—the power of God, 'which giveth us the victory through our Lord Jesus Christ.' 1 Corinthians 15:57.

"He who grasps this thought has before him an infinite field for study. He has the key that will unlock to him the whole treasure house of God's word" (*Education,* pp. 125, 126).

And as we contemplate this truth, we can also see the reason, the logic, and the truth in the following statement. "There is but little benefit derived from a hasty reading of the Scriptures. One may read the whole Bible through and yet fail to see its beauty or comprehend its deep and hidden meaning. One passage studied until its significance is clear to the mind and its relation to the plan of salvation is evident, is of more value than the perusal of many chapters with no definite purpose in view and no positive instruction gained" (*Steps to Christ,* p. 90).

As we study inspiration we find so clearly outlined the cosmic struggle between God and Satan, good and evil, righteousness and unrighteousness, and we learn of the mighty plan of God and His only Son, Jesus, to provide a means of escape from the curse and consequence of sin. How true the word that he who understands that God's covenant to redeem man is the central theme of the Bible has "the key that will unlock to him the whole treasure house of God's word."

So, dear reader, it is the deep, earnest, candid study of the new covenant, the plan of redemption—the foundation of the Christian's faith—and its application to our hearts and lives that is the first goal and purpose of this book. The second goal and purpose is to gain a deep understanding of the pillars of our faith that, along with the foundation, give solidity and strength to our faith. May you study each subject through the lens, the magnifying glass of the new covenant, God's wonderful plan of redemption, to restore in the human soul His own image. May God be with you as you read, and may the Holy Spirit be your Teacher and Guide.

"For God so loved the world that He gave His only begotten Son,
that whoever believes in Him should not perish but have everlasting life."
John 3:16

"The central theme of the Bible, the theme about which every
other in the whole book clusters, is the redemption plan,
the restoration in the human soul of the image of God."
Education, pp. 125, 126

Chapter 1
The Foundation – The New Covenant

1 Corinthians 3:11
"For no other foundation can anyone lay than that which is laid, which is Jesus Christ."

Psalm 111:9
"He has sent redemption to His people; He has commanded His covenant forever: Holy and awesome is His name."

Zechariah 6:13
"Yes, He shall build the temple of the Lord. He shall bear the glory, and shall sit and rule on His throne; so He shall be a priest on His throne, and the counsel of peace shall be between them both."

Revelation 13:8
"All who dwell on the earth will worship him, whose names have not been written in the Book of Life of the Lamb slain from the foundation of the world."

John 3:16
"For God so loved the world that He gave His only begotten Son, that whoever believes in Him should not perish but have everlasting life."

Patriarchs and Prophets, p. 63
"The Son of God, heaven's glorious Commander, was touched with pity for the fallen race. His heart was moved with infinite compassion as the woes of the lost world rose up before Him. But divine love had conceived a plan whereby man might be redeemed. The broken law of God demanded the life of the sinner. In all the universe there was but one who could, in behalf of man, satisfy its claims. Since the divine law is as sacred as God Himself, only one equal with God could make atonement for its transgression. None but Christ could redeem fallen man from the curse of the law and bring him again into harmony with Heaven. Christ would take upon Himself the guilt and shame of sin—sin so offensive to a holy God that it must separate the Father and His Son. Christ would reach to the depths of misery to rescue the ruined race.

"Before the Father He pleaded in the sinner's behalf, while the host of heaven awaited the result with an intensity of interest that words cannot express. Long continued was that mysterious communing—'the counsel of peace' (Zechariah 6:13) for the fallen sons of men. The plan of salvation had been laid before the creation of the earth; for Christ is 'the Lamb slain from the foundation of the world' (Revelation 13:8); yet it was a struggle, even with the King of the universe, to yield up His Son to die for the guilty race. But 'God so loved the world, that He gave His only-begotten Son, that whosoever believeth in Him should not perish, but have everlasting life.' John 3:16."

2 Corinthians 5:15–21
"And He died for all, that those who live should live no longer for themselves, but for Him who died for them and rose again.

"Therefore, from now on, we regard no one according to the flesh. Even though we have known Christ according to the flesh, yet now we know *Him thus* no longer. Therefore, if anyone *is* in Christ, *he is* a new creation; old things have passed away; behold, all things have become new. Now all things *are* of God, who has reconciled us to Himself through Jesus Christ, and has given us the ministry of reconciliation, that is, that God was in Christ reconciling the world to Himself, not imputing their trespasses to them, and has committed to us the word of reconciliation.

"Now then, we are ambassadors for Christ, as though God were pleading through us: we implore *you* on Christ's behalf, be reconciled to God. For He made Him who knew no sin *to be* sin for us, that we might become the righteousness of God in Him."

1 John 3:2
"Beloved, now we are children of God; and it has not yet been revealed what we shall be, but we know that when He is revealed, we shall be like Him, for we shall see Him as He is."

Hebrews 1:14
"Are they not all ministering spirits sent forth to minister for those who will inherit salvation?"

Hebrews 2:18
"For in that He Himself has suffered, being tempted, He is able to aid those who are tempted."

Hebrews 2:9
"But we see Jesus, who was made a little lower than the angels, for the suffering of death crowned with glory and honor, that He, by the grace of God, might taste death for everyone."

Patriarchs and Prophets, pp. 64, 65
"God was to be manifest in Christ, 'reconciling the world unto Himself.' 2 Corinthians 5:19. Man had become so degraded by sin that it was impossible for him, in himself, to come into harmony with Him whose nature is purity and goodness. But Christ, after having redeemed man from the condemnation of the law, could impart divine power to unite with human effort. Thus by repentance toward God and faith in Christ the fallen children of Adam might once more become 'sons of God.' 1 John 3:2.

"The plan by which alone man's salvation could be secured, involved all heaven in its infinite sacrifice. The angels could not rejoice as Christ opened before them the plan of redemption, for they saw that man's salvation must cost their loved Commander unutterable woe. In grief and wonder they listened to His words as He told them how He must descend from heaven's purity and peace, its joy and glory and immortal life, and come in contact with the degradation of earth, to endure its sorrow, shame, and death. He was to stand between the sinner and the penalty of sin; yet few would receive Him as the Son of God. He would leave His high position as the Majesty of heaven, appear upon earth and humble Himself as a man, and by His own experience become acquainted with the sorrows and temptations which man would have to endure. All this would be necessary in order that He might be able to succor them that should be tempted. Hebrews 2:18. When His mission as a teacher should be ended, He must be delivered into the hands of wicked men and be subjected to every insult and torture that Satan could inspire them to inflict. He must die the cruelest of deaths, lifted up between the heavens and the earth as a guilty sinner. He must pass long hours of agony so terrible that angels could not look upon it, but would veil their faces from the sight. He must endure anguish of soul, the hiding of His Father's face, while the guilt of transgression—the weight of the sins of the whole world—should be upon Him.

"The angels prostrated themselves at the feet of their Commander and offered to become a sacrifice for man. But an angel's life could not pay the debt; only He who created man had power to redeem him. Yet the angels were to have a part to act in the plan of redemption. Christ was to be made 'a little lower than the angels for the suffering of death.' Hebrews 2:9. As He should take human nature upon Him, His strength would not be equal to theirs, and they were to minister to Him, to strengthen and soothe Him under His sufferings. They were also to be ministering spirits, sent forth to minister for them who should be heirs of salvation. Hebrews 1:14. They would guard the subjects of grace from the power of evil angels and from the darkness constantly thrown around them by Satan.

"When the angels should witness the agony and humiliation of their Lord, they would be filled with grief and indignation and would wish to deliver Him from His murderers; but they were not to interpose in order to prevent anything which they should behold. It was a part of the plan of redemption that Christ should suffer the scorn and abuse of wicked men, and He consented to all this when He became the Redeemer of man.

"Christ assured the angels that by His death He would ransom many, and would destroy him who had the power of death. He would recover the kingdom which man had lost by transgression, and the redeemed were to inherit it with Him, and dwell therein forever. Sin and sinners would be blotted out, nevermore to disturb the peace of heaven or earth. He bade the angelic host to be in accord with the plan that His Father had accepted, and

rejoice that, through His death, fallen man could be reconciled to God."

Genesis 3:15
"And I will put enmity between you and the woman, and between your seed and her Seed; He shall bruise your head, and you shall bruise His heel."

***Patriarchs and Prophets*, pp. 65, 66**
"To man the first intimation of redemption was communicated in the sentence pronounced upon Satan in the garden. The Lord declared, 'I will put enmity between thee and the woman, and between thy seed and her seed; it shall bruise thy head, and thou shalt bruise his heel.' Genesis 3:15. This sentence, uttered in the hearing of our first parents, was to them a promise. While it foretold war between man and Satan, it declared that the power of the great adversary would finally be broken. Adam and Eve stood as criminals before the righteous Judge, awaiting the sentence which transgression had incurred; but before they heard of the life of toil and sorrow which must be their portion, or of the decree that they must return to dust, they listened to words that could not fail to give them hope. Though they must suffer from the power of their mighty foe, they could look forward to final victory."

John 12:31, 32
"Now is the judgment of this world; now the ruler of this world will be cast out. And I, if I am lifted up from the earth, will draw all *peoples* to Myself."

***Patriarchs and Prophets*, pp. 68, 69**
"But the plan of redemption had a yet broader and deeper purpose than the salvation of man. It was not for this alone that Christ came to

the earth; it was not merely that the inhabitants of this little world might regard the law of God as it should be regarded; but it was to vindicate the character of God before the universe. To this result of His great sacrifice—its influence upon the intelligences of other worlds, as well as upon man—the Saviour looked forward when just before His crucifixion He said: 'Now is the judgment of this world: now shall the prince of this world be cast out. And I, if I be lifted up from the earth, will draw all unto Me.' John 12:31, 32. The act of Christ in dying for the salvation of man would not only make heaven accessible to men, but before all the universe it would justify God and His Son in their dealing with the rebellion of Satan. It would establish the perpetuity of the law of God and would reveal the nature and the results of sin."

Genesis 22:18
"In your seed all the nations of the earth shall be blessed, because you have obeyed My voice."

Galatians 3:8, 16
"And the Scripture, foreseeing that God would justify the Gentiles by faith, preached the gospel to Abraham beforehand, *saying*, 'In you all the nations shall be blessed.' ... Now to Abraham and his Seed were the promises made. He does not say, 'And to seeds,' as of many, but as of one, 'And to your Seed,' who is Christ."

Genesis 17:1
"When Abram was ninety-nine years old, the Lord appeared to Abram and said to him, 'I *am* Almighty God; walk before Me and be blameless.' "

Genesis 26:5
"Because Abraham obeyed My voice and kept My charge, My commandments, My statutes, and My laws."

Genesis 17:7
"And I will establish My covenant between Me and you and your descendants after you in their generations, for an everlasting covenant, to be God to you and your descendants after you."

> "This covenant... was simply an arrangement for bringing men again into harmony with the divine will, placing them where they could obey God's law."

Patriarchs and Prophets, pp. 370, 371
"The covenant of grace was first made with man in Eden, when after the Fall there was given a divine promise that the seed of the woman should bruise the serpent's head. To all men this covenant offered pardon and the assisting grace of God for future obedience through faith in Christ. It also promised them eternal life on condition of fidelity to God's law. Thus the patriarchs received the hope of salvation.

"This same covenant was renewed to Abraham in the promise, 'In thy seed shall all the nations of the earth be blessed.' Genesis 22:18. This promise pointed to Christ. So Abraham understood it (see Galatians 3:8, 16), and he trusted in Christ for the forgiveness of sins. It was this faith that was accounted unto him for righteousness. The covenant with Abraham also maintained the authority of God's law. The Lord appeared unto Abraham, and said, 'I am the Almighty God; walk before Me, and be thou perfect.' Genesis 17:1. The testimony of God concerning His faithful servant was, 'Abraham obeyed My voice, and kept My charge, My commandments, My statutes, and My laws.' Genesis 26:5. And the Lord declared to him, 'I will establish My covenant between Me and thee and thy seed after thee in their generations, for an *everlasting covenant*, to be a God unto thee and to thy seed after thee.' Genesis 17:7.

"Though this covenant was made with Adam and renewed to Abraham, it could not be ratified until the death of Christ. It had existed by the promise of God since the first intimation of redemption had been given; it had been accepted by faith; yet when ratified by Christ, it is called a *new* covenant. The law of God was the basis of this covenant, which was simply an arrangement for bringing men again into harmony with the divine will, placing them where they could obey God's law."

Romans 16:25

"Now to Him who is able to establish you according to my gospel and the preaching of Jesus Christ, according to the revelation of the mystery kept secret since the world began."

The Desire of Ages, p. 22

"The plan for our redemption was not an afterthought, a plan formulated after the fall of Adam. It was a revelation of 'the mystery which hath been kept in silence through times eternal.' Romans 16:25, R. V. It was an unfolding of the principles that from eternal ages have been the foundation of God's throne. From the beginning, God and Christ knew of the apostasy of Satan, and of the fall of man through the deceptive power of the apostate. God did not ordain that sin should exist, but He foresaw its existence, and made provision

to meet the terrible emergency. So great was His love for the world, that He covenanted to give His only-begotten Son, "that whosoever believeth in Him should not perish, but have everlasting life." John 3:16."

> "So great was His love for the world, that He covenanted to give His only-begotten Son, 'that whosoever believeth in Him should not perish, but have everlasting life.'"

Isaiah 53:7

"He was oppressed and He was afflicted, yet He opened not His mouth; He was led as a lamb to the slaughter, and as a sheep before its shearers is silent, so He opened not His mouth."

John 1:29–34

"The next day John saw Jesus coming toward him, and said, 'Behold! The Lamb of God who takes away the sin of the world! This is He of whom I said, "After me comes a Man who is preferred before me, for He was before me." I did not know Him; but that He should be revealed to Israel, therefore I came baptizing with water.'

"And John bore witness, saying, 'I saw the Spirit descending from heaven like a dove, and He remained upon Him. I did not know Him, but He who sent me to baptize with water said to me, "Upon whom you see the Spirit descending, and remaining on Him, this is He who baptizes with the Holy Spirit." And I have seen and testified that this is the Son of God.' "

The Desire of Ages, pp. 136, 137

"When at the baptism of Jesus, John pointed to Him as the Lamb of God, a new light was shed upon the Messiah's work. The prophet's mind was directed to the words of Isaiah, 'He is brought as a lamb to the slaughter.' Isaiah 53:7. During the weeks that followed, John with new interest studied the prophecies and the teaching of the sacrificial service. He did not distinguish clearly the two phases of Christ's work,—as a suffering sacrifice and a conquering king,—but he saw that His coming had a deeper significance than priests or people had discerned. When he beheld Jesus among the throng on His return from the desert, he confidently looked for Him to give the people some sign of His true character. Almost impatiently he waited to hear the Saviour declare His mission; but no word was spoken, no sign given. Jesus did not respond to the Baptist's announcement of Him, but mingled with the disciples of John, giving no outward evidence of His special work, and taking no measures to bring Himself to notice.

"The next day John sees Jesus coming. With the light of the glory of God resting upon him, the prophet stretches out his hands, declaring, 'Behold the Lamb of God, which taketh away the sin of the world! This is He of whom I said, After me cometh a man which is become before me…. And I knew Him not; but that He should be made manifest to Israel, for this cause came I baptizing in water…. I have beheld the Spirit descending as a dove out of heaven; and it abode upon Him. And I knew Him not: but He that sent me to baptize in water, He said unto me, Upon whomsoever thou shalt see the Spirit descending, and abiding upon Him, the same is He that baptizeth with the Holy Spirit. And I have seen, and have borne witness that this is the Son of God.' John 1:29–34, R. V., margin."

Hebrews 8:1, 2

"Now *this is* the main point of the things we are saying: We have such a High Priest, who is seated at the right hand of the throne of the Majesty in the heavens, a Minister of the sanctuary and of the true tabernacle which the Lord erected, and not man."

The Great Controversy, p. 413

" 'Now of the things which we have spoken this is the sum: We have such an High Priest, who is set on the right hand of the throne of the Majesty in the heavens; a Minister of the sanctuary, and of the true tabernacle, which the Lord pitched, and not man.' Hebrews 8:1, 2.

"Here is revealed the sanctuary of the new covenant."

Revelation 7:9, 10

"After these things I looked, and behold, a great multitude which no one could number, of all nations, tribes, peoples, and tongues, standing before the throne and before the Lamb, clothed with white robes, with palm branches in their hands, and crying out with a loud voice, saying, 'Salvation *belongs* to our God who sits on the throne, and to the Lamb!' "

The Great Controversy, p. 665

"Now Christ again appears to the view of His enemies. Far above the city, upon a foundation of burnished gold, is a throne, high and lifted up. Upon this throne sits the Son of God, and around Him are the subjects of His kingdom. The power and majesty of Christ no language can describe, no pen portray. The glory of the Eternal Father is enshrouding His Son. The brightness of His presence fills the City of God, and flows out beyond the gates, flooding the whole earth with its radiance.

"Nearest the throne are those who were once zealous in the cause of Satan, but who, plucked as brands from the burning, have followed their Saviour with deep, intense devotion. Next are those who perfected Christian characters in the midst of falsehood and infidelity, those who honored the law of God when the Christian world declared it void, and the millions, of all ages, who were martyred for their faith. And beyond is the 'great multitude, which no man could number, of all nations, and kindreds, and people, and tongues, ... before the throne, and before the Lamb, clothed with white robes, and palms in their hands.' Revelation 7:9. Their warfare is ended, their victory won. They have run the race and reached the prize. The palm branch in their hands is a symbol of their triumph, the white robe an emblem of the spotless righteousness of Christ which now is theirs.

"The redeemed raise a song of praise that echoes and re-echoes through the vaults of heaven: 'Salvation to our God which sitteth upon the throne, and unto the Lamb.' Verse 10. And angel and seraph unite their voices in adoration. As the redeemed have beheld the power and malignity of Satan, they have seen, as never before, that no power but that of Christ could have made them conquerors. In all that shining throng there are none to ascribe salvation to themselves, as if they had prevailed by their own power and goodness. Nothing is said of what they have done or suffered; but the burden of every song, the keynote of every anthem, is: Salvation to our God and unto the Lamb."

Revelation 5:12

"Saying with a loud voice: 'Worthy is the Lamb who was slain to receive power and riches and wisdom, and strength and honor and glory and blessing!' "

The Great Controversy, p. 671

"Before the universe has been clearly presented the great sacrifice made by the Father and the Son in man's behalf. The hour has come when Christ occupies His rightful position and is glorified above principalities and powers and every name that is named. It was for the joy that was set before Him—that He might bring many sons unto glory—that He endured the cross and despised the shame. And inconceivably great as was the sorrow and the shame, yet greater is the joy and the glory. He looks upon the redeemed, renewed in His own image, every heart bearing the perfect impress of the divine, every face reflecting the likeness of their King. He beholds in them the result of the travail of His soul, and He is satisfied. Then, in a voice that reaches the assembled multitudes of the righteous and the wicked, He declares: 'Behold the purchase of My blood! For these I suffered, for these I died, that they might dwell in My presence throughout eternal ages.' And the song of praise ascends from the white-robed ones about the throne: 'Worthy is the Lamb that was slain to receive power, and riches, and wisdom, and strength, and honor, and glory, and blessing.' Revelation 5:12."

Revelation 21:1

"Now I saw a new heaven and a new earth, for the first heaven and the first earth had passed away. Also there was no more sea."

Habakkuk 3:4

"*His* brightness was like the light; He had rays *flashing* from His hand, and there His power *was* hidden."

Isaiah 63:1

"Who *is* this who comes from Edom, with dyed garments from Bozrah, This *One who is* glorious in His apparel, traveling in the greatness of His strength?— 'I who speak in righteousness, mighty to save.' "

The Great Controversy, p. 674

" 'I saw a new heaven and a new earth: for the first heaven and the first earth were passed away.' Revelation 21:1. The fire that consumes the wicked purifies the earth. Every trace of the curse is swept away. No eternally burning hell will keep before the ransomed the fearful consequences of sin.

"One reminder alone remains: Our Redeemer will ever bear the marks of His crucifixion. Upon His wounded head, upon His side, His hands and feet, are the only traces of the cruel work that sin has wrought. Says the prophet, beholding Christ in His glory: 'He had bright beams coming out of His side: and there was the hiding of His power.' Habakkuk 3:4, margin. That pierced side whence flowed the crimson stream that reconciled man to God—there is the Saviour's glory, there 'the hiding of His power.' 'Mighty to save [Isaiah 63:1],' through the sacrifice of redemption, He was therefore strong to execute justice upon them that despised God's mercy. And the tokens of His humiliation are His highest honor; through the eternal ages the wounds of Calvary will show forth His praise and declare His power."

The Great Controversy, p. 678

"The great controversy is ended. Sin and sinners are no more. The entire universe is clean. One pulse of harmony and gladness beats through the vast creation. From Him who created all, flow life and light and gladness, throughout the realms of illimitable space. From the minutest atom to the greatest world, all things, animate and inanimate, in their unshadowed beauty and perfect joy, declare that God is love."

Psalm 77:13

"Your way, O God, *is* in the sanctuary; who *is* so great a God as *our* God?"

Psalm 150:1

"Praise the Lord! Praise God in His sanctuary; praise Him in His mighty firmament!"

"We have such a High Priest, who is seated at the right hand of the
throne of the Majesty in the heavens, a Minister of the sanctuary
and of the true tabernacle which the Lord erected, and not man."
Hebrews 8:1, 2

"The intercession of Christ in man's behalf in the sanctuary above
is as essential to the plan of salvation as was His death upon the cross."
The Great Controversy, p. 489

Chapter 2

The Sanctuary of the New Covenant

Hebrews 8:1, 2

"Now *this is* the main point of the things we are saying: we have such a High Priest, who is seated at the right hand of the throne of the Majesty in the heavens, a Minister of the sanctuary and of the true tabernacle which the Lord erected, and not man."

The Great Controversy, p. 413

" 'Now of the things which we have spoken this is the sum: We have such an High Priest, who is set on the right hand of the throne of the Majesty in the heavens; a Minister of the sanctuary, and of the true tabernacle, which the Lord pitched, and not man.' Hebrews 8:1, 2.

"Here is revealed the sanctuary of the new covenant."

Daniel 8:14

"And he said to me, 'For two thousand three hundred days; then the sanctuary shall be cleansed.' "

The Great Controversy, p. 417

"The question, What is the sanctuary? is clearly answered in the Scriptures. The term 'sanctuary,' as used in the Bible, refers, first, to the tabernacle built by Moses, as a pattern of heavenly things; and, secondly, to the 'true tabernacle' in heaven, to which the earthly sanctuary pointed. At the death of Christ the typical service ended. The 'true tabernacle' in heaven is the sanctuary of the new covenant. And as the prophecy of Daniel 8:14 is fulfilled in this dispensation, the sanctuary to which it refers must be the sanctuary of the new covenant. At the termination of the 2300 days, in 1844, there had been no sanctuary on earth for many centuries. Thus the prophecy, 'Unto two thousand and three hundred days; then shall the sanctuary be cleansed,' unquestionably points to the sanctuary in heaven."

> "The 'true tabernacle' in heaven is the sanctuary of the new covenant."

Hebrews 9:9

"It *was* symbolic for the present time in which both gifts and sacrifices are offered which cannot make him who performed the service perfect in regard to the conscience."

Hebrews 9:23, 24

"Therefore *it was* necessary that the copies of the things in the heavens should be purified with these, but the heavenly things themselves with better sacrifices than these. For Christ has not entered the holy places made with hands, *which are* copies of the true, but into heaven itself, now to appear in the presence of God for us."

Revelation 4:5

"And from the throne proceeded lightnings, thunderings, and voices. Seven lamps of fire *were* burning before the throne, which are the seven Spirits of God."

Revelation 8:3

"Then another angel, having a golden censer, came and stood at the altar. He was given much incense, that he should offer *it* with the prayers of all the saints upon the golden altar which was before the throne."

Revelation 11:19

"Then the temple of God was opened in heaven, and the ark of His covenant was seen in His temple. And there were lightnings, noises, thunderings, an earthquake, and great hail."

Patriarchs and Prophets, p. 356

"As has been stated, the earthly sanctuary was built by Moses according to the pattern shown him in the mount. It was 'a figure for the time then present, in which were offered both gifts and sacrifices;' its two holy places were 'patterns of things in the heavens;' Christ, our great High Priest, is 'a minister of the sanctuary, and of the true tabernacle, which the Lord pitched, and not man.' Hebrews 9:9, 23; 8:2. As in vision the apostle John was granted a view of the temple of God in heaven, he beheld there 'seven lamps of fire burning before the throne.' He saw an angel 'having a golden censer; and there was given unto him much incense, that he should offer it with the prayers of all saints upon the golden altar which was before the throne.' Revelation 4:5; 8:3. Here the prophet was permitted to behold the first apartment of the sanctuary in heaven; and he saw there the 'seven lamps of fire' and the 'golden altar' represented by the golden candlestick and the altar of incense in the sanctuary on earth. Again, 'the temple of God was opened' (Revelation 11:19), and he looked within the inner veil, upon the holy of holies. Here he beheld 'the ark of His testament' (Revelation 11:19), represented by the sacred chest constructed by Moses to contain the law of God."

Hebrews 9:1–3

"Then indeed, even the first *covenant* had ordinances of divine service and the earthly sanctuary. For a tabernacle was prepared: the first *part*, in which *was* the lampstand, the table, and the showbread, which is called the sanctuary; and behind the second veil, the part of the tabernacle which is called the Holiest of All."

Exodus 25:9, 40

"According to all that I show you, *that is*, the pattern of the tabernacle and the pattern of all its furnishings, just so you shall make *it*."

"And see to it that you make *them* according to the pattern which was shown you on the mountain."

Hebrews 8:5

"Who serve the copy and shadow of the heavenly things, as Moses was divinely instructed when he was about to make the tabernacle. For He said, 'See *that* you make all things according to the pattern shown you on the mountain.' "

The Great Controversy, pp. 412–414

"After the settlement of the Hebrews in Canaan, the tabernacle was replaced by the temple of Solomon, which, though a permanent structure and upon a larger scale, observed the same proportions, and was similarly furnished. In this form the sanctuary existed—except while it lay in ruins in Daniel's time—until its destruction by the Romans, in A.D. 70.

"This is the only sanctuary that ever existed on the earth, of which the Bible gives any information. This was declared by Paul to be the sanctuary of the first covenant. But has the new covenant no sanctuary?

"Turning again to the book of Hebrews, the seekers for truth found that the existence of a second, or new-covenant sanctuary, was implied in the words of Paul already quoted: 'Then verily the first covenant had *also* ordinances of divine service, and a worldly sanctuary [Hebrews 9:1].' And the use of the word 'also' intimates that Paul has before made mention of this sanctuary. Turning back to the beginning of the previous chapter, they read: 'Now of the things which we have spoken this is the sum: We have such an High Priest, who is set on the right hand of the throne of the Majesty in the heavens; a Minister of the sanctuary, and of the true tabernacle, which the Lord pitched, and not man.' Hebrews 8:1, 2.

"Here is revealed the sanctuary of the new covenant. The sanctuary of the first covenant was pitched by man, built by Moses; this is pitched by the Lord, not by man. In that sanctuary the earthly priests performed their service; in this, Christ, our great High Priest, ministers at God's right hand. One sanctuary was on earth, the other is in heaven.

"Further, the tabernacle built by Moses was made after a pattern. The Lord directed him: 'According to all that I show thee, after the pattern of the tabernacle, and the pattern of all the instruments thereof, even so shall ye make it.' And again the charge was given, 'Look that thou make them after their pattern, which was showed thee in the mount.' Exodus 25:9, 40. And Paul says that the first tabernacle 'was a figure for the time then present, in which were offered both gifts and sacrifices;' that its holy places were 'patterns of things in the heavens;' that the priests who offered gifts according to the law served 'unto the example and shadow of heavenly things,' and that 'Christ is not entered into the holy places made with hands, which are the figures of the true; but into heaven itself, now to appear in the presence of God for us.' Hebrews 9:9, 23; 8:5; 9:24.

"The sanctuary in heaven, in which Jesus ministers in our behalf, is the great original, of which the sanctuary built by Moses was a copy."

Daniel 7:10

"A fiery stream issued and came forth from before Him. A thousand thousands ministered to Him; ten thousand times ten thousand stood before Him. The court was seated, and the books were opened."

The Great Controversy, pp. 414, 415

"The matchless splendor of the earthly tabernacle reflected to human vision the glories of that heavenly temple where Christ our forerunner ministers for us before the throne of God. The abiding place of the King of kings, where thousand thousands minister unto Him, and ten thousand times ten thousand stand before Him (Daniel 7:10); that temple, filled with the glory of the eternal throne, where seraphim, its shining guardians, veil their faces in adoration, could find, in the most magnificent structure ever reared by human hands, but a faint reflection of its vastness and glory. Yet important truths concerning the heavenly sanctuary and the great work there carried forward for man's redemption were taught by the earthly sanctuary and its services.

"The holy places of the sanctuary in heaven are represented by the two apartments in the sanctuary on earth. As in vision the apostle John was granted a view of the temple of God in heaven, he beheld there 'seven lamps of fire burning before the throne.' Revelation 4:5. He saw an angel 'having a golden censer; and there was given unto him much incense, that he should offer it with the prayers of all saints upon the golden altar which was before the throne.' Revelation 8:3. Here the prophet was permitted to behold the first apartment of the sanctuary in heaven; and he saw there the 'seven lamps of fire' and 'the golden altar,' represented by the golden candlestick and the altar of incense in the sanctuary on earth. Again, 'the temple of God was opened' (Revelation 11:19), and he looked within the inner veil, upon the holy of holies. Here he beheld 'the ark of His testament,' represented by the sacred chest constructed by Moses to contain the law of God.

"Thus those who were studying the subject found indisputable proof of the existence of a sanctuary in heaven. Moses made the earthly sanctuary after a pattern which was shown him. Paul teaches that that pattern was the true sanctuary which is in heaven. And John testifies that he saw it in heaven.

"In the temple in heaven, the dwelling place of God, His throne is established in righteousness and judgment. In the most holy place is His law, the great rule of right by which all mankind are tested. The ark that enshrines the tables of the law is covered with the mercy seat, before which Christ pleads His blood in the sinner's behalf."

> ## "The sanctuary in heaven is the very center of Christ's work in behalf of men... It opens to view the plan of redemption"

The Great Controversy, p. 488
"Those who would share the benefits of the Saviour's mediation should permit nothing to interfere with their duty to perfect holiness in the fear of God. The precious hours, instead of being given to pleasure, to display, or to gain seeking, should be devoted to an earnest, prayerful study of the word of truth.

The subject of the sanctuary and the investigative judgment should be clearly understood by the people of God. All need a knowledge for themselves of the position and work of their great High Priest. Otherwise it will be impossible for them to exercise the faith which is essential at this time or to occupy the position which God designs them to fill."

The Great Controversy, pp. 488, 489
"All who have received the light upon these subjects are to bear testimony of the great truths which God has committed to them. The sanctuary in heaven is the very center of Christ's work in behalf of men. It concerns every soul living upon the earth. It opens to view the plan of redemption, bringing us down to the very close of time and revealing the triumphant issue of the contest between righteousness and sin. It is of the utmost importance that all should thoroughly investigate these subjects and be able to give an answer to everyone that asketh them a reason of the hope that is in them.

"The intercession of Christ in man's behalf in the sanctuary above is as essential to the plan of salvation as was His death upon the cross. By His death He began that work which after His resurrection He ascended to complete in heaven."

The Great Controversy, p. 423
"The subject of the sanctuary was the key which unlocked the mystery of the disappointment of 1844. It opened to view a complete system of truth, connected and harmonious, showing that God's hand had directed the great advent movement and revealing present duty as it brought to light the position and work of His people.... Now in the holy of holies they again beheld Him, their compassionate High Priest, soon to appear as their king and

deliverer. Light from the sanctuary illumined the past, the present, and the future. They knew that God had led them by His unerring providence."

"The intercession of Christ in man's behalf in the sanctuary above is as essential to the plan of salvation as was His death upon the cross."

Evangelism, p. 221

"The correct understanding of the ministration in the heavenly sanctuary is the foundation of our faith."

Counsels on Sabbath School Work, pp. 12, 13

"The Sabbath school should be a place where the jewels of truth are searched for and rescued from their environment of error, and placed in their true setting in the framework of the gospel. Precious gems of truth, long lost sight of, are now to be restored to the children of God. The themes of justification by faith, the righteousness of Christ, should be presented in our schools, that the youth and children may understand these important subjects, and teachers and scholars may know the way of salvation. Sacred and eternal principles connected with the plan of salvation have long been lost from sight, but they must be restored to their proper place in the plan of salvation, and made to appear in their heavenly light, and penetrate the moral darkness in which the world is enshrouded."

Matthew 25:1–13

"Then the kingdom of heaven shall be likened to ten virgins who took their lamps and went out to meet the bridegroom. Now five of them were wise, and five *were* foolish. Those who *were* foolish took their lamps and took no oil with them, but the wise took oil in their vessels with their lamps. But while the bridegroom was delayed, they all slumbered and slept.

"And at midnight a cry was *heard*: 'Behold, the bridegroom is coming; go out to meet him!' Then all those virgins arose and trimmed their lamps. And the foolish said to the wise, 'Give us *some* of your oil, for our lamps are going out.' But the wise answered, saying, '*No*, lest there should not be enough for us and you; but go rather to those who sell, and buy for yourselves.' And while they went to buy, the bridegroom came, and those who were ready went in with him to the wedding; and the door was shut.

"Afterward the other virgins came also, saying, 'Lord, Lord, open to us!' But he answered and said, 'Assuredly, I say to you, I do not know you.'

"Watch therefore, for you know neither the day nor the hour in which the Son of Man is coming."

The Great Controversy, pp. 427, 428

"In the parable it was those that had oil in their vessels with their lamps that went in to the marriage. Those who, with a knowledge of the truth from the Scriptures, had also the Spirit and grace of God, and who, in the night of their bitter trial, had patiently waited, searching the Bible for clearer light—these saw the truth concerning the sanctuary in heaven and the Saviour's change in ministration, and by faith they followed Him in His work in the sanctuary above. And all who through the testimony of the Scriptures accept the same truths, following Christ by faith as He enters in before God to perform the last work of mediation, and at its close to receive His kingdom—all these are represented as going in to the marriage."

The Great Controversy, pp. 393, 394

"The parable of the ten virgins of Matthew 25 also illustrates the experience of the Adventist people. In Matthew 24 … He spoke of His coming in His kingdom, and related the parable [verses 45–51] describing the two classes of servants who look for His appearing. Chapter 25 opens with the words: 'Then shall the kingdom of heaven be likened unto ten virgins.' Here is brought to view the church living in the last days, the same that is pointed out in the close of chapter 24. In this parable their experience is illustrated by the incidents of an Eastern marriage.

" 'Then shall the kingdom of heaven be likened unto ten virgins, which took their lamps, and went forth to meet the bridegroom. And five of them were wise, and five were foolish. They that were foolish took their lamps, and took no oil with them: but the wise took oil in their vessels with their lamps. While the bridegroom tarried, they all slumbered and slept. And at midnight there was a cry made, Behold, the bridegroom cometh; go ye out to meet him.'

"The coming of Christ, as announced by the first angel's message, was understood to be represented by the coming of the bridegroom. The widespread reformation under the proclamation of His soon coming, answered to the going forth of the virgins. In this parable, as in that of Matthew 24, two classes are represented. All had taken their lamps, the Bible, and by its light had gone forth to meet the Bridegroom. But while 'they that were foolish took their lamps, and took no oil with them,' 'the wise took oil in their vessels with their lamps.' The latter class had received the grace of God, the regenerating, enlightening power of the Holy Spirit, which renders His word a lamp to the feet and a light to the path. In the fear of God they had studied the Scriptures to learn the truth, and had earnestly sought for purity of heart and life. These had a personal experience, a faith in God and in His word, which could not be overthrown by disappointment and delay. Others 'took their lamps, and took no oil with them.' They had moved from impulse. Their fears had been excited by the solemn message, but they had depended upon the faith of their brethren, satisfied with the flickering light of good emotions, without a thorough understanding of the truth or a genuine work of grace in the heart. These had gone forth to meet the Lord, full of hope in the prospect of immediate reward; but they were not prepared for delay and disappointment. When trials came, their faith failed, and their lights burned dim."

Evangelism, p. 223

"Our faith in reference to the messages of the first, second, and third angels [Revelation 14:6-12] was correct. The great way-marks we have passed are immovable. Although the hosts of hell may try to tear them from their foundation, and triumph in the thought that they have succeeded, yet they do not succeed. These pillars of truth stand firm as the eternal hills, unmoved by all the efforts of men combined with those of Satan and his host. We can learn much, and should be constantly searching the Scriptures to see if these things are so. God's people are now to have their eyes fixed on the heavenly sanctuary, where the final ministration of our great High Priest in the work of the judgment is going forward,—where he is interceding for his people."

Revelation 14:12

"Here is the patience of the saints; here *are* those who keep the commandments of God and the faith of Jesus."

The Great Controversy, **pp. 593, 594**

"Those who endeavor to obey all the commandments of God will be opposed and derided. They can stand only in God. In order to endure the trial before them, they must understand the will of God as revealed in His word; they can honor Him only as they have a right conception of His character, government, and purposes, and act in accordance with them. None but those who have fortified the mind with the truths of the Bible will stand through the last great conflict. To every soul will come the searching test: Shall I obey God rather than men? The decisive hour is even now at hand. Are our feet planted on the rock of God's immutable word? Are we prepared to stand firm in defense of the commandments of God and the faith of Jesus [Revelation 14:12]?"

Evangelism, **pp. 222, 223**

"As a people, we should be earnest students of prophecy; we should not rest until we become intelligent in regard to the subject of the sanctuary, which is brought out in the visions of Daniel and John. This subject sheds great light on our present position and work, and gives us unmistakable proof that God has led us in our past experience. It explains our disappointment in 1844, showing us that the sanctuary to be cleansed was not the earth, as we had supposed, but that Christ then entered into the most holy apartment of the heavenly sanctuary, and is there performing the closing work of his priestly office, in fulfillment of the words of the angel to the prophet Daniel,

'Unto two thousand and three hundred days; then shall the sanctuary be cleansed.' "

The Great Controversy, **p. 417**

"At the death of Christ the typical service ended. The 'true tabernacle' in heaven is the sanctuary of the new covenant. And as the prophecy of Daniel 8:14 is fulfilled in this dispensation, the sanctuary to which it refers must be the sanctuary of the new covenant. At the termination of the 2300 days, in 1844, there had been no sanctuary on earth for many centuries. Thus the prophecy, 'Unto two thousand and three hundred days; then shall the sanctuary be cleansed,' unquestionably points to the sanctuary in heaven."

Evangelism, **pp. 224, 225**

"The time is near when the deceptive powers of satanic agencies will be fully developed. On one side is Christ, who has been given all power in heaven and earth. On the other side is Satan, continually exercising his power to allure, to deceive with strong, spiritualistic sophistries, to remove God out of the places that He should occupy in the minds of men.

"Satan is striving continually to bring in fanciful suppositions in regard to the sanctuary, degrading the wonderful representations of God and the ministry of Christ for our salvation into something that suits the carnal mind. He removes its presiding power from the hearts of believers, and supplies its place with fantastic theories invented to make void the truths of the atonement, and destroy our confidence in the doctrines which we have held sacred since the third angel's message was first given. Thus he would rob us of our faith in the very message that has made us a separate people, and has given character and power to our work."

"He said to me, 'For 2,300 evenings *and* mornings;
then the holy place will be properly restored.'"
Daniel 8:14 NASB

"The scripture which above all others had been both the foundation and the
central pillar of the advent faith was the declaration: 'Unto two thousand
and three hundred days; then shall the sanctuary be cleansed.' Daniel 8:14."
The Great Controversy, p. 409

Chapter 3

The Foundation and Central Pillar – Daniel 8:14

Daniel 8:14

"And he said to me, 'For two thousand three hundred days; then the sanctuary shall be cleansed.' "

***The Great Controversy*, p. 409**

"The scripture which above all others had been both the foundation and the central pillar of the advent faith was the declaration: 'Unto two thousand and three hundred days; then shall the sanctuary be cleansed.' Daniel 8:14."

Exodus 25:8, 9, 40

"And let them make Me a sanctuary, that I may dwell among them. According to all that I show you, *that is*, the pattern of the tabernacle and the pattern of all its furnishings, just so you shall make *it*."

"And see to it that you make *them* according to the pattern which was shown you on the mountain."

Acts 7:44

"Our fathers had the tabernacle of witness in the wilderness, as He appointed, instructing Moses to make it according to the pattern that he had seen."

Hebrews 6:17–20

"Thus God, determining to show more abundantly to the heirs of promise the immutability of His counsel, confirmed *it* by an oath, that by two immutable things, in which *it* is impossible for God to lie, we might have strong consolation, who have fled for refuge to lay hold of the hope set before *us*.

"This *hope* we have as an anchor of the soul, both sure and steadfast, and which enters the *Presence* behind the veil, where the forerunner has entered for us, *even* Jesus, having become High Priest forever according to the order of Melchizedek."

***Patriarchs and Prophets*, p. 371**

"The Abrahamic covenant was ratified by the blood of Christ, and it is called the 'second,' or 'new,' covenant, because the blood by which it was sealed was shed after the blood of the first covenant. That the new covenant was valid in the days of Abraham is evident from the fact that it was then confirmed both by the promise and by the oath of God—the 'two immutable things, in which it was impossible for God to lie.' Hebrews 6:18."

Hebrews 7:15–28

"And it is yet far more evident if, in the likeness of Melchizedek, there arises another priest who has come, not according to the law of a fleshly commandment, but according to the power of an endless life. For He testifies: 'You *are* a priest forever according to the order of Melchizedek.'

"For on the one hand there is an annulling of the former commandment because of its weakness and unprofitableness, for the law made nothing perfect; on the other hand, *there is the* bringing in of a better hope, through which we draw near to God.

"And inasmuch as *He was* not *made priest* without an oath (for they have become priests without an oath, but He with an oath by Him who said to Him: 'The Lord has sworn and will not relent, "You *are* a priest forever according to the order of Melchizedek" '), by so much more Jesus has become a surety of a better covenant.

"Also there were many priests, because they were prevented by death from continuing. But He, because He continues forever, has an unchangeable priesthood. Therefore He is also able to save to the uttermost those who come to God through Him, since He always lives to make intercession for them.

"For such a High Priest was fitting for us, *who is* holy, harmless, undefiled, separate from sinners, and has become higher than the heavens; who does not need daily, as those high priests, to offer up sacrifices, first for His own sins and then for the people's, for this He did once for all when He offered up Himself. For the law appoints as high priests men who have weakness, but the word of the oath, which came after the law, *appoints* the Son who has been perfected forever."

Hebrews 8:1–6

"Now *this is* the main point of the things we are saying: we have such a High Priest, who is seated at the right hand of the throne of the Majesty in the heavens, a Minister of the sanctuary and of the true tabernacle which the Lord erected, and not man.

"For every high priest is appointed to offer both gifts and sacrifices. Therefore *it is* necessary that this One also have something to offer. For if He were on earth, He would not be a priest, since there are priests who offer the gifts according to the law; who serve the copy and shadow of the heavenly things, as Moses was divinely instructed when he was about to make the tabernacle. For He said, 'See *that* you make all things according to the pattern shown you on the mountain.' But now He has

obtained a more excellent ministry, inasmuch as He is also Mediator of a better covenant, which was established on better promises."

The Great Controversy, p. 413

" 'Now of the things which we have spoken this is the sum: We have such an High Priest, who is set on the right hand of the throne of the Majesty in the heavens; a Minister of the sanctuary, and of the true tabernacle, which the Lord pitched, and not man.' Hebrews 8:1, 2.

"Here is revealed the sanctuary of the new covenant. The sanctuary of the first covenant was pitched by man, built by Moses; this is pitched by the Lord, not by man. In that sanctuary the earthly priests performed their service; in this, Christ, our great High Priest, ministers at God's right hand. One sanctuary was on earth, the other is in heaven."

Hebrews 9:1–5

"Then indeed, even the first *covenant* [the word *covenant* is not in the original manuscript] had ordinances of divine service and the earthly sanctuary. For a tabernacle was prepared: the first *part*, in which *was* the lampstand, the table, and the showbread, which is called the sanctuary; and behind the second veil, the part of the tabernacle which is called the Holiest of All, which had the golden censer and the ark of the covenant overlaid on all sides with gold, in which *were* the golden pot that had the manna, Aaron's rod that budded, and the tablets of the covenant; and above it were the cherubim of glory overshadowing the mercy seat. Of these things we cannot now speak in detail."

The Great Controversy, p. 411

"The sanctuary to which Paul here refers was the tabernacle built by Moses at the command of God as the earthly dwelling place of the

Most High. 'Let them make Me a sanctuary; that I may dwell among them' (Exodus 25:8)."

Hebrews 9:6–15
"Now when these things had been thus prepared, the priests always went into the first part of the tabernacle, performing *the services*. But into the second part the high priest *went* alone once a year, not without blood, which he offered for himself and *for* the people's sins *committed* in ignorance; the Holy Spirit indicating this, that the way into the Holiest of All was not yet made manifest while the first tabernacle was still standing. It *was* symbolic for the present time in which both gifts and sacrifices are offered which cannot make him who performed the service perfect in regard to the conscience—*concerned* only with foods and drinks, various washings, and fleshly ordinances imposed until the time of reformation.

"But Christ came as High Priest of the good things to come, with the greater and more perfect tabernacle not made with hands, that is, not of this creation. Not with the blood of goats and calves, but with His own blood He entered the Most Holy Place once for all, having obtained eternal redemption. For if the blood of bulls and goats and the ashes of a heifer, sprinkling the unclean, sanctifies for the purifying of the flesh, how much more shall the blood of Christ, who through the eternal Spirit offered Himself without spot to God, cleanse your conscience from dead works to serve the living God? And for this reason He is the Mediator of the new covenant, by means of death, for the redemption of the transgressions under the first covenant, that those who are called may receive the promise of the eternal inheritance."

Hebrews 9:21–24
"Then likewise he sprinkled with blood both the tabernacle and all the vessels of the ministry. And according to the law almost all things are purified with blood, and without shedding of blood there is no remission.

"Therefore *it was* necessary that the copies of the things in the heavens should be purified with these, but the heavenly things themselves with better sacrifices than these. For Christ has not entered the holy places made with hands, *which are* copies of the true, but into heaven itself, now to appear in the presence of God for us."

Patriarchs and Prophets, **pp. 356, 357**
"As has been stated, the earthly sanctuary was built by Moses according to the pattern shown him in the mount. It was 'a figure for the time then present, in which were offered both gifts and sacrifices;' its two holy places were 'patterns of things in the heavens;' Christ, our great High Priest, is 'a minister of the sanctuary, and of the true tabernacle, which the Lord pitched, and not man.' Hebrews 9:9, 23; 8:2....

"Moses made the earthly sanctuary, 'according to the fashion that he had seen.' Paul declares that 'the tabernacle, and all the vessels of the ministry,' when completed, were 'the patterns of things in the heavens.' Acts 7:44; Hebrews 9:21, 23. And John says that he saw the sanctuary in heaven. That sanctuary, in which Jesus ministers in our behalf, is the great original, of which the sanctuary built by Moses was a copy."

The Great Controversy, **pp. 413, 417**
"The Lord directed him: 'According to all that I show thee, after the pattern of the tabernacle, and the pattern of all the instruments thereof, even so shall ye make it.' And again the charge

was given, 'Look that thou make them after their pattern, which was showed thee in the mount.' Exodus 25:9, 40. And Paul says that the first tabernacle 'was a figure for the time then present, in which were offered both gifts and sacrifices;' that its holy places were 'patterns of things in the heavens;' that the priests who offered gifts according to the law served 'unto the example and shadow of heavenly things,' and that 'Christ is not entered into the holy places made with hands, which are the figures of the true; but into heaven itself, now to appear in the presence of God for us.' Hebrews 9:9, 23; 8:5; 9:24."

"In Hebrews 9 the cleansing of both the earthly and the heavenly sanctuary is plainly taught. 'Almost all things are by the law purged with blood; and without shedding of blood is no remission. It was therefore necessary that the patterns of things in the heavens should be purified with these [the blood of animals]; but the heavenly things themselves with better sacrifices than these' (Hebrews 9:22, 23), even the precious blood of Christ."

Hebrews 9:25–28

"Not that He should offer Himself often, as the high priest enters the Most Holy Place every year with blood of another—He then would have had to suffer often since the foundation of the world; but now, once at the end of the ages, He has appeared to put away sin by the sacrifice of Himself. And as it is appointed for men to die once, but after this the judgment, so Christ was offered once to bear the sins of many. To those who eagerly wait for Him He will appear a second time, apart from sin, for salvation."

The Great Controversy, p. 423

"The subject of the sanctuary was the key which unlocked the mystery of the disappointment of 1844. It opened to view a complete system of truth, connected and harmonious, showing that God's hand had directed the great advent movement and revealing present duty as it brought to light the position and work of His people.... Now in the holy of holies they again beheld Him, their compassionate High Priest, soon to appear as their king and deliverer. Light from the sanctuary illumined the past, the present, and the future. They knew that God had led them by His unerring providence."

> ## "The subject of the sanctuary … opened to view a complete system of truth, connected and harmonious."

The Great Controversy, p. 489

"The intercession of Christ in man's behalf in the sanctuary above is as essential to the plan of salvation as was His death upon the cross. By His death He began that work which after His resurrection He ascended to complete in heaven. We must by faith enter within the veil, 'whither the forerunner is for us entered.' Hebrews 6:20. There the light from the cross of Calvary is reflected. There we may gain a clearer insight into the mysteries of redemption. The salvation of man is accomplished at an infinite expense to heaven; the sacrifice made is equal to the broadest demands of the broken law of God. Jesus has opened the way to the Father's throne, and through His mediation the sincere desire of all who come to Him in faith may be presented before God."

Daniel 8:9–14

"And out of one of them came a little horn which grew exceedingly great toward the south, toward the east, and toward the Glorious *Land*. And it grew up to the host of heaven; and it cast down *some* of the host and *some* of the stars to the ground, and trampled them. He even exalted *himself* as high as the Prince of the host; and by him the daily *sacrifices* were taken away, and the place of His sanctuary was cast down. Because of transgression, an army was given over *to the horn* to oppose the daily *sacrifices*; and he cast truth down to the ground. He did *all this* and prospered.

"Then I heard a holy one speaking; and *another* holy one said to that certain *one* who was speaking, 'How long *will* the vision *be, concerning* the daily *sacrifices* and the transgression of desolation, the giving of both the sanctuary and the host to be trampled underfoot?'

"And he said to me, 'For two thousand three hundred days; then the sanctuary shall be cleansed.' "

"Light from the sanctuary illumined the past, the present, and the future. They knew that God had led them by His unerring providence."

Early Writings, pp. 74, 75
"Then I saw in relation to the 'daily' (Daniel 8:12) that the word 'sacrifice' was supplied by man's wisdom, and does not belong to the text, and that the Lord gave the correct view of it to those who gave the judgment hour cry."

Daniel 8:14, NASB
"He said to me, 'For 2,300 evenings *and* mornings; then the holy place will be properly restored.' "

Daniel 8:14, RSV
"And he said to him, 'For two thousand and three hundred evenings and mornings; then the sanctuary shall be restored to its rightful state.' "

Daniel 8:14, NIV
"He said to me, 'It will take 2,300 evenings and mornings; then the sanctuary will be reconsecrated.' "

Ezekiel 37:26–28
"Moreover I will make a covenant of peace with them, and it shall be an everlasting covenant with them; I will establish them and multiply them, and I will set My sanctuary in their midst forevermore. My tabernacle also shall be with them; indeed I will be their God, and they shall be My people. The nations also will know that I, the Lord, sanctify Israel, when My sanctuary is in their midst forevermore."

Christ Opens the Holy Place of the Sanctuary in Heaven

John 20:16, 17
"Jesus said to her, 'Mary!' She turned and said to Him, 'Rabboni!' (which is to say, Teacher). Jesus said to her, 'Do not cling to Me, for I have not yet ascended to My Father; but go to My brethren and say to them, "I am ascending to My Father and your Father, and *to* My God and your God." ' "

Isaiah 13:12
"I will make a mortal more rare than fine gold, a man more than the golden wedge of Ophir."

The Desire of Ages, p. 790
"But now in His own familiar voice Jesus said to her, 'Mary.' Now she knew that it was not a stranger who was addressing her, and turning

she saw before her the living Christ. In her joy she forgot that He had been crucified. Springing toward Him, as if to embrace His feet, she said, 'Rabboni.' But Christ raised His hand, saying, Detain Me not; 'for I am not yet ascended to My Father: but go to My brethren, and say unto them, I ascend unto My Father, and your Father; and to My God, and your God [John 20:16, 17].' And Mary went her way to the disciples with the joyful message.

"Jesus refused to receive the homage of His people until He had the assurance that His sacrifice was accepted by the Father. He ascended to the heavenly courts, and from God Himself heard the assurance that His atonement for the sins of men had been ample, that through His blood all might gain eternal life. The Father ratified the covenant made with Christ, that He would receive repentant and obedient men, and would love them even as He loves His Son. Christ was to complete His work, and fulfill His pledge to 'make a man more precious than fine gold; even a man than the golden wedge of Ophir.' Isaiah 13:12. All power in heaven and on earth was given to the Prince of Life, and He returned to His followers in a world of sin, that He might impart to them of His power and glory."

The Acts of the Apostles, pp. 38, 39

"Christ's ascension to heaven was the signal that His followers were to receive the promised blessing. For this they were to wait before they entered upon their work. When Christ passed within the heavenly gates, He was enthroned amidst the adoration of the angels. As soon as this ceremony was completed, the Holy Spirit descended upon the disciples in rich currents, and Christ was indeed glorified, even with the glory which He had with the Father from all eternity. The Pentecostal outpouring was Heaven's communication that the Redeemer's inauguration was accomplished. According to His promise He had sent the Holy Spirit from heaven to His followers as a token that He had, as priest and king, received all authority in heaven and on earth, and was the Anointed One over His people."

Revelation 4:1–11

"After these things I looked, and behold, a door *standing* open in heaven. And the first voice which I heard *was* like a trumpet speaking with me, saying, 'Come up here, and I will show you things which must take place after this.'

"Immediately I was in the Spirit; and behold, a throne set in heaven, and *One* sat on the throne. And He who sat there was like a jasper and a sardius stone in appearance; and *there was* a rainbow around the throne, in appearance like an emerald. Around the throne *were* twenty-four thrones, and on the thrones I saw twenty-four elders sitting, clothed in white robes; and they had crowns of gold on their heads. And from the throne proceeded lightnings, thunderings, and voices. Seven lamps of fire *were* burning before the throne, which are the seven Spirits of God.

"Before the throne *there was* a sea of glass, like crystal. And in the midst of the throne, and around the throne, *were* four living creatures full of eyes in front and in back. The first living creature *was* like a lion, the second living creature like a calf, the third living creature had a face like a man, and the fourth living creature *was* like a flying eagle. *The* four living creatures, each having six wings, were full of eyes around and within. And they do not rest day or night, saying: 'Holy, holy, holy, Lord God Almighty, Who was and is and is to come!'

"Whenever the living creatures give glory and honor and thanks to Him who sits on the throne, who lives forever and ever, the twenty-four elders fall down before Him who sits on the throne and worship Him who lives forever and ever, and cast their crowns before the throne, saying: 'You are worthy, O Lord, To receive glory and honor and power; for You created all things, and by Your will they exist and were created.' "

Revelation 5:1–14
"And I saw in the right *hand* of Him who sat on the throne a scroll written inside and on the back, sealed with seven seals. Then I saw a strong angel proclaiming with a loud voice, 'Who is worthy to open the scroll and to loose its seals?' And no one in heaven or on the earth or under the earth was able to open the scroll, or to look at it.

"So I wept much, because no one was found worthy to open and read the scroll, or to look at it. But one of the elders said to me, 'Do not weep. Behold, the Lion of the tribe of Judah, the Root of David, has prevailed to open the scroll and to loose its seven seals.'

"And I looked, and behold, in the midst of the throne and of the four living creatures, and in the midst of the elders, stood a Lamb as though it had been slain, having seven horns and seven eyes, which are the seven Spirits of God sent out into all the earth. Then He came and took the scroll out of the right hand of Him who sat on the throne.

"Now when He had taken the scroll, the four living creatures and the twenty-four elders fell down before the Lamb, each having a harp, and golden bowls full of incense, which are the prayers of the saints. And they sang a new song, saying: 'You are worthy to take the scroll, and to open its seals; for You were slain, and have redeemed us to God by Your blood out of every tribe and tongue and people and nation, and have made us kings and priests to our God; and we shall reign on the earth.'

"Then I looked, and I heard the voice of many angels around the throne, the living creatures, and the elders; and the number of them was ten thousand times ten thousand, and thousands of thousands, saying with a loud voice: 'Worthy is the Lamb who was slain to receive power and riches and wisdom, and strength and honor and glory and blessing!'

"And every creature which is in heaven and on the earth and under the earth and such as are in the sea, and all that are in them, I heard saying: 'Blessing and honor and glory and power *be* to Him who sits on the throne, and to the Lamb, forever and ever!'

"Then the four living creatures said, 'Amen!' And the twenty-four elders fell down and worshiped Him who lives forever and ever."

Revelation 1:12–16
"Then I turned to see the voice that spoke with me. And having turned I saw seven golden lampstands, and in the midst of the seven lampstands *One* like the Son of Man, clothed with a garment down to the feet and girded about the chest with a golden band. His head and hair *were* white like wool, as white as snow, and His eyes like a flame of fire; His feet *were* like fine brass, as if refined in a furnace, and His voice as the sound of many waters; He had in His right hand seven stars, out of His mouth went a sharp two-edged sword, and His countenance *was* like the sun shining in its strength."

Matthew 28:20
" 'Teaching them to observe all things that I have commanded you; and lo, I am with you always, *even* to the end of the age.' Amen."

The Desire of Ages, pp. 830, 831

"Upon reaching the Mount of Olives, Jesus led the way across the summit, to the vicinity of Bethany. Here He paused, and the disciples gathered about Him. Beams of light seemed to radiate from His countenance as He looked lovingly upon them. He upbraided them not for their faults and failures; words of the deepest tenderness were the last that fell upon their ears from the lips of their Lord. With hands outstretched in blessing, and as if in assurance of His protecting care, He slowly ascended from among them, drawn heavenward by a power stronger than any earthly attraction. As He passed upward, the awe-stricken disciples looked with straining eyes for the last glimpse of their ascending Lord. A cloud of glory hid Him from their sight; and the words came back to them as the cloudy chariot of angels received Him, 'Lo, I am with you alway, even unto the end of the world [Matthew 28:20].' At the same time there floated down to them the sweetest and most joyous music from the angel choir."

The Desire of Ages, p. 832

"Christ had ascended to heaven in the form of humanity. The disciples had beheld the cloud receive Him. The same Jesus who had walked and talked and prayed with them; who had broken bread with them; who had been with them in their boats on the lake; and who had that very day toiled with them up the ascent of Olivet,—the same Jesus had now gone to share His Father's throne."

The Desire of Ages, p. 833

"All heaven was waiting to welcome the Saviour to the celestial courts. As He ascended, He led the way, and the multitude of captives set free at His resurrection followed. The heavenly host, with shouts and acclamations of praise and celestial song, attended the joyous train."

John 19:30

"So when Jesus had received the sour wine, He said, 'It is finished!' and bowing His head, He gave up His spirit."

John 17:24

"Father, I desire that they also whom You gave Me may be with Me where I am, that they may behold My glory which You have given Me; for You loved Me before the foundation of the world."

Ephesians 1:6

"To the praise of the glory of His grace, by which He made us accepted in the Beloved."

Psalm 85:10

"Mercy and truth have met together; righteousness and peace have kissed."

Hebrews 1:6

"But when He again brings the firstborn into the world, He says: 'Let all the angels of God worship Him.' "

Revelation 5:12, 13

"Saying with a loud voice: 'Worthy is the Lamb who was slain to receive power and riches and wisdom, and strength and honor and glory and blessing!' And every creature which is in heaven and on the earth and under the earth and such as are in the sea, and all that are in them, I heard saying: 'Blessing and honor and glory and power *be* to Him who sits on the throne, and to the Lamb, forever and ever!' "

***The Desire of Ages*, pp. 833–835**

"Then the portals of the city of God are opened wide, and the angelic throng sweep through the gates amid a burst of rapturous music.

"There is the throne, and around it the rainbow of promise. There are cherubim and seraphim. The commanders of the angel hosts, the sons of God, the representatives of the unfallen worlds, are assembled. The heavenly council before which Lucifer had accused God and His Son, the representatives of those sinless realms over which Satan had thought to establish his dominion,—all are there to welcome the Redeemer. They are eager to celebrate His triumph and to glorify their King.

"But He waves them back. Not yet; He cannot now receive the coronet of glory and the royal robe. He enters into the presence of His Father. He points to His wounded head, the pierced side, the marred feet; He lifts His hands, bearing the print of nails. He points to the tokens of His triumph; He presents to God the wave sheaf, those raised with Him as representatives of that great multitude who shall come forth from the grave at His second coming. He approaches the Father, with whom there is joy over one sinner that repents; who rejoices over one with singing. Before the foundations of the earth were laid, the Father and the Son had united in a covenant to redeem man if he should be overcome by Satan. They had clasped Their hands in a solemn pledge that Christ should become the surety for the human race. This pledge Christ has fulfilled. When upon the cross He cried out, 'It is finished,' He addressed the Father. The compact had been fully carried out. Now He declares: Father, it is finished. I have done Thy will, O My God. I have completed the work of redemption. If Thy justice is satisfied, 'I will that they also, whom Thou hast given Me, be with Me where I am.' John 19:30; 17:24.

"The voice of God is heard proclaiming that justice is satisfied. Satan is vanquished. Christ's toiling, struggling ones on earth are 'accepted in the Beloved.' Ephesians 1:6. Before the heavenly angels and the representatives of unfallen worlds, they are declared justified. Where He is, there His church shall be. 'Mercy and truth are met together; righteousness and peace have kissed each other.' Psalm 85:10. The Father's arms encircle His Son, and the word is given, 'Let all the angels of God worship Him.' Hebrews 1:6.

"With joy unutterable, rulers and principalities and powers acknowledge the supremacy of the Prince of life. The angel host prostrate themselves before Him, while the glad shout fills all the courts of heaven, 'Worthy is the Lamb that was slain to receive power, and riches, and wisdom, and strength, and honor, and glory, and blessing.' Revelation 5:12.

"Songs of triumph mingle with the music from angel harps, till heaven seems to overflow with joy and praise. Love has conquered. The lost is found. Heaven rings with voices in lofty strains proclaiming, 'Blessing, and honor, and glory, and power, be unto Him that sitteth upon the throne, and unto the Lamb forever and ever.' Revelation 5:13."

Christ Opens the Most Holy Place of the Sanctuary in Heaven

Revelation 3:7, 8

"And to the angel of the church in Philadelphia write, 'These things says He who is holy, He who is true, "He who has the key of David, He who opens and no one shuts, and shuts and no one opens": "I know your works. See, I have set before you an open door, and no one can shut it; for you have a little strength, have kept My word, and have not denied My name." ' "

The Great Controversy, p. 429, 430

"They [Adventists in 1844] now saw that they were correct in believing that the end of the 2300 days in 1844 marked an important crisis. But while it was true that that door of hope and mercy by which men had for eighteen hundred years found access to God, was closed, another door was opened, and forgiveness of sins was offered to men through the intercession of Christ in the most holy. One part of His ministration had closed, only to give place to another. There was still an 'open door' to the heavenly sanctuary, where Christ was ministering in the sinner's behalf.

"Now was seen the application of those words of Christ in the Revelation, addressed to the church at this very time: 'These things saith He that is holy, He that is true, He that hath the key of David, He that openeth, and no man shutteth; and shutteth, and no man openeth; I know thy works: behold, I have set before thee an open door, and no man can shut it.' Revelation 3:7, 8."

Revelation 11:15–19

"Then the seventh angel sounded: and there were loud voices in heaven, saying, 'The kingdoms of this world have become *the kingdoms* of our Lord and of His Christ, and He shall reign forever and ever!' And the twenty-four elders who sat before God on their thrones fell on their faces and worshiped God, saying:

" 'We give You thanks, O Lord God Almighty, the One who is and who was and who is to come, because You have taken Your great power and reigned. The nations were angry, and Your wrath has come, and the time of the dead, that they should be judged, and that You should reward Your servants the prophets and the saints, and those who fear Your name, small and great, and should destroy those who destroy the earth.'

"Then the temple of God was opened in heaven, and the ark of His covenant was seen in His temple. And there were lightnings, noises, thunderings, an earthquake, and great hail."

The Great Controversy, p. 433

" 'The temple of God was opened in heaven, and there was seen in His temple the ark of His testament.' Revelation 11:19. The ark of God's testament is in the holy of holies, the second apartment of the sanctuary. In the ministration of the earthly tabernacle, which served 'unto the example and shadow of heavenly things [Hebrews 8:5],' this apartment was opened only upon the great Day of Atonement for the cleansing of the sanctuary. Therefore the announcement that the temple of God was opened in heaven and the ark of His testament was seen points to the opening of the most holy place of the heavenly sanctuary in 1844 as Christ entered there to perform the closing work of the atonement."

Daniel 7:9, 10, 13, 14

"I watched till thrones were put in place, and the Ancient of Days was seated; His garment *was* white as snow, and the hair of His head *was* like pure wool. His throne *was* a fiery flame, its wheels a burning fire; a fiery stream issued and came forth from before Him. A thousand thousands ministered to Him; ten thousand times ten thousand stood before Him. The court was seated, and the books were opened."

"I was watching in the night visions, and behold, *One* like the Son of Man, coming with the clouds of heaven! He came to the Ancient of Days, and they brought Him near before Him. Then to Him was given dominion and glory and a kingdom, that all peoples, nations, and languages should serve Him. His dominion *is* an everlasting dominion, which shall not pass away, And His kingdom *the one* which shall not be destroyed.”

Matthew 16:27

“For the Son of Man will come in the glory of His Father with His angels, and then He will reward each according to his works.”

The Great Controversy, p. 479

“ ‘I beheld,’ says the prophet Daniel, ‘till thrones were placed, and One that was Ancient of Days did sit: His raiment was white as snow, and the hair of His head like pure wool; His throne was fiery flames, and the wheels thereof burning fire. A fiery stream issued and came forth from before Him: thousand thousands ministered unto Him, and ten thousand times ten thousand stood before Him: the judgment was set, and the books were opened.’ Daniel 7:9, 10, R.V.

“Thus was presented to the prophet’s vision the great and solemn day when the characters and the lives of men should pass in review before the Judge of all the earth, and to every man should be rendered ‘according to his works [Matthew 16:27].’ The Ancient of Days is God the Father.”

The Great Controversy, pp. 479, 480

“ ‘And, behold, one like the Son of man came with the clouds of heaven, and came to the Ancient of Days, and they brought Him near before Him. And there was given Him dominion, and glory, and a kingdom, that all people, nations, and languages, should serve Him: His dominion is an everlasting dominion, which shall not pass away.’ Daniel 7:13, 14. The coming of Christ here described is not His second coming to the earth. He comes to the Ancient of Days in heaven to receive dominion and glory and a kingdom, which will be given Him

at the close of His work as a mediator. It is this coming, and not His second advent to the earth, that was foretold in prophecy to take place at the termination of the 2300 days in 1844.”

Revelation 10:1, 2, 7

“I saw still another mighty angel coming down from heaven, clothed with a cloud. And a rainbow *was* on his head, his face *was* like the sun, and his feet like pillars of fire. He had a little book open in his hand. And he set his right foot on the sea and *his* left *foot* on the land.”

“But in the days of the sounding of the seventh angel, when he is about to sound, the mystery of God would be finished, as He declared to His servants the prophets.”

Manuscript Releases, vol. 1, p. 99

“The mighty angel who instructed John was no less a personage than Jesus Christ. Setting His right foot on the sea, and His left upon the dry land, shows the part which He is acting in the closing scenes of the the great controversy with Satan. This position denotes His supreme power and authority over the whole earth.”

Malachi 3:1–3

“ ‘Behold, I send My messenger, and he will prepare the way before Me. And the Lord, whom you seek, will suddenly come to His temple, even the Messenger of the covenant, in whom you delight. Behold, He is coming,’ says the Lord of hosts.

“But who can endure the day of His coming? And who can stand when He appears? For He *is* like a refiner’s fire and like launderers’ soap. He will sit as a refiner and a purifier of silver; He will purify the sons of Levi, and purge them as gold and silver, that they may offer to the Lord an offering in righteousness.”

The Great Controversy, p. 425

"Says the prophet: 'Who may abide the day of His coming? and who shall stand when He appeareth? for He is like a refiner's fire, and like fullers' soap: and He shall sit as a refiner and purifier of silver: and He shall purify the sons of Levi, and purge them as gold and silver, that they may offer unto the Lord an offering in righteousness.' Malachi 3:2, 3. Those who are living upon the earth when the intercession of Christ shall cease in the sanctuary above are to stand in the sight of a holy God without a mediator. Their robes must be spotless, their characters must be purified from sin by the blood of sprinkling. Through the grace of God and their own diligent effort they must be conquerors in the battle with evil. While the investigative judgment is going forward in heaven, while the sins of penitent believers are being removed from the sanctuary, there is to be a special work of purification, of putting away of sin, among God's people upon earth. This work is more clearly presented in the messages of Revelation 14."

Revelation 14:6, 7

"Then I saw another angel flying in the midst of heaven, having the everlasting gospel to preach to those who dwell on the earth—to every nation, tribe, tongue, and people—saying with a loud voice, 'Fear God and give glory to Him, for the hour of His judgment has come; and worship Him who made heaven and earth, the sea and springs of water.' "

The Great Controversy, p. 355

"A Great religious awakening under the proclamation of Christ's soon coming is foretold in the prophecy of the first angel's message of Revelation 14. An angel is seen flying 'in the midst of heaven, having the everlasting gospel to preach unto them that dwell on the earth, and to every nation, and kindred, and tongue, and people.' 'With a loud voice' he proclaims the message: 'Fear God, and give glory to Him; for the hour of His judgment is come: and worship Him that made heaven, and earth, and the sea, and the fountains of waters.' [Revelation 14] Verses 6, 7."

The Great Controversy, pp. 355, 356

"The message itself sheds light as to the time when this movement is to take place. It is declared to be a part of the 'everlasting gospel;' and it announces the opening of the judgment. The message of salvation has been preached in all ages; but this message is a part of the gospel which could be proclaimed only in the last days, for only then would it be true that the hour of judgment *had come*."

The Great Controversy, p. 424

"Both the prophecy of Daniel 8:14, 'Unto two thousand and three hundred days; then shall the sanctuary be cleansed,' and the first angel's message, 'Fear God, and give glory to Him; for the hour of His judgment is come [Revelation 14:7],' pointed to Christ's ministration in the most holy place, to the investigative judgment."

Matthew 25:1–13

"Then the kingdom of heaven shall be likened to ten virgins who took their lamps and went out to meet the bridegroom. Now five of them were wise, and five *were* foolish. Those who *were* foolish took their lamps and took no oil with them, but the wise took oil in their vessels with their lamps. But while the bridegroom was delayed, they all slumbered and slept.

"And at midnight a cry was *heard*: 'Behold, the bridegroom is coming; go out to meet him!' Then all those virgins arose and trimmed their lamps. And the foolish said to the wise, 'Give us *some* of your oil, for our lamps are going out.' But the wise answered, saying, '*No*, lest there should not be enough for us and you; but go rather to those who sell, and buy for yourselves.' And while they went to buy, the bridegroom came, and those who were ready went in with him to the wedding; and the door was shut.

"Afterward the other virgins came also, saying, 'Lord, Lord, open to us!' But he answered and said, 'Assuredly, I say to you, I do not know you.'

"Watch therefore, for you know neither the day nor the hour in which the Son of Man is coming."

Revelation 21:9, 10

"Then one of the seven angels who had the seven bowls filled with the seven last plagues came to me and talked with me, saying, 'Come, I will show you the bride, the Lamb's wife.' And he carried me away in the Spirit to a great and high mountain, and showed me the great city, the holy Jerusalem, descending out of heaven from God."

The Great Controversy, pp. 426, 427

"The coming of the bridegroom, here brought to view, takes place before the marriage. The marriage represents the reception by Christ of His kingdom. The Holy City, the New Jerusalem, which is the capital and representative of the kingdom, is called 'the bride, the Lamb's wife.' Said the angel to John: 'Come hither, I will show thee the bride, the Lamb's wife.' 'He carried me away in the spirit,' says the prophet, 'and showed me that great city, the holy Jerusalem, descending out of heaven from God.' Revelation 21:9, 10."

The Great Controversy, pp. 427, 428

"In the parable it was those that had oil in their vessels with their lamps that went in to the marriage. Those who, with a knowledge of the truth from the Scriptures, had also the Spirit and grace of God, and who, in the night of their bitter trial, had patiently waited, searching the Bible for clearer light—these saw the truth concerning the sanctuary in heaven and the Saviour's change in ministration, and by faith they followed Him in His work in the sanctuary above. And all who through the testimony of the Scriptures accept the same truths, following Christ by faith as He enters in before God to perform the last work of mediation, and at its close to receive His kingdom—all these are represented as going in to the marriage....

"When the work of investigation shall be ended, when the cases of those who in all ages have professed to be followers of Christ have been examined and decided, then, and not till then, probation will close, and the door of mercy will be shut. Thus in the one short sentence, 'They that were ready went in with Him to the marriage: and the door was shut [Matthew 25:10],' we are carried down through the Saviour's final ministration, to the time when the great work for man's salvation shall be completed."

Matthew 22:1–14

"And Jesus answered and spoke to them again by parables and said: 'The kingdom of heaven is like a certain king who arranged a marriage for his son, and sent out his servants to call those who were invited to the wedding; and they were not willing to come. Again, he sent out other servants, saying, "Tell those who are invited, 'See, I have prepared my dinner; my oxen and fatted cattle *are* killed, and all things *are* ready. Come to the wedding.' " But they made light of it and went their ways, one to his own farm, another to his business. And the rest seized his servants, treated *them* spitefully, and killed *them*. But when the king heard *about it*, he was furious. And he sent out his armies, destroyed those murderers, and burned up their city. Then he said to his servants, "The wedding is ready, but those who were invited were not worthy. Therefore go into the highways, and as many as you find, invite to the wedding." So those servants went out into the highways and gathered together all whom they found, both bad and good. And the wedding *hall* was filled with guests.

" 'But when the king came in to see the guests, he saw a man there who did not have on a wedding garment. So he said to him, "Friend, how did you come in here without a wedding garment?" And he was speechless. Then the king said to the servants, "Bind him hand and foot, take him away, and cast *him* into outer darkness; there will be weeping and gnashing of teeth."

" 'For many are called, but few *are* chosen.' "

Revelation 7:14
"And I said to him, 'Sir, you know.' So he said to me, 'These are the ones who come out of the great tribulation, and washed their robes and made them white in the blood of the Lamb.' "

The Great Controversy, p. 428
"In the parable of Matthew 22 the same figure of the marriage is introduced, and the investigative judgment is clearly represented as taking place before the marriage. Previous to the wedding the king comes in to see the guests, to see if all are attired in the wedding garment, the spotless robe of character washed and made white in the blood of the Lamb. Matthew 22:11; Revelation 7:14. He

who is found wanting is cast out, but all who upon examination are seen to have the wedding garment on are accepted of God and accounted worthy of a share in His kingdom and a seat upon His throne. This work of examination of character, of determining who are prepared for the kingdom of God, is that of the investigative judgment, the closing of work in the sanctuary above."

Revelation 14:15
"And another angel came out of the temple, crying with a loud voice to Him who sat on the cloud, 'Thrust in Your sickle and reap, for the time has come for You to reap, for the harvest of the earth is ripe.' "

The Great Controversy, pp. 311, 312
"To prepare a people to stand in the day of God, a great work of reform was to be accomplished. God saw that many of His professed people were not building for eternity, and in His mercy He was about to send a message of warning to arouse them from their stupor and lead them to make ready for the coming of the Lord.

"This warning is brought to view in Revelation 14 [verses 6–12]. Here is a three-fold message represented as proclaimed by heavenly beings and immediately followed by the coming of the Son of man to reap 'the harvest of the earth [Revelation 14:15].' The first of these warnings announces the approaching judgment. The prophet beheld an angel flying 'in the midst of heaven, having the everlasting gospel to preach unto them that dwell on the earth, and to every nation, and kindred, and tongue, and people, saying with a loud voice, Fear God, and give glory to Him; for the hour of His judgment is come: and worship Him that made heaven, and earth, and the sea, and the fountains of waters.' Revelation 14:6, 7.

"This message is declared to be a part of 'the everlasting gospel.' "

A Parallel

***Early Writings*, pp. 259–261**

"I was pointed back to the proclamation of the first advent of Christ. John was sent in the spirit and power of Elijah to prepare the way of Jesus. Those who rejected the testimony of John were not benefited by the teachings of Jesus. Their opposition to the message that foretold His coming placed them where they could not readily receive the strongest evidence that He was the Messiah. Satan led on those who rejected the message of John to go still farther, to reject and crucify Christ. In doing this they placed themselves where they could not receive the blessing on the day of Pentecost, which would have taught them the way into the heavenly sanctuary. The rending of the veil of the temple showed that the Jewish sacrifices and ordinances would no longer be received. The great Sacrifice had been offered and had been accepted, and the Holy Spirit which descended on the day of Pentecost carried the minds of the disciples from the earthly sanctuary to the heavenly, where Jesus had entered by His own blood, to shed upon His disciples the benefits of His atonement. But the Jews were left in total darkness. They lost all the light which they might have had upon the plan of salvation, and still trusted in their useless sacrifices and offerings. The heavenly sanctuary had taken the place of the earthly, yet they had no knowledge of the change. Therefore they could not be benefited by the mediation of Christ in the holy place.

"Many look with horror at the course of the Jews in rejecting and crucifying Christ; and as they read the history of His shameful abuse, they think they love Him, and would not have denied Him as did Peter, or crucified Him as did the Jews. But God who reads the hearts of all, has brought to the test that love for Jesus which they professed to feel. All heaven watched with the deepest interest the reception of the first angel's message. But many who professed to love Jesus, and who shed tears as they read the story of the cross, derided the good news of His coming. Instead of receiving the message with gladness, they declared it to be a delusion. They hated those who loved His appearing and shut them out of the churches."

Daniel 8:14, NASB

"He said to me, 'For 2,300 evenings *and* mornings; then the holy place will be properly restored.'

"The law of the LORD is perfect, converting the soul; ... Moreover by them
Your servant is warned, and in keeping them there is great reward."
Psalm 19:7, 11

"The law of God in the sanctuary in heaven is the great original....
The law of God, being a revelation of His will,
a transcript of His character, must forever endure."
The Great Controversy, p. 434

Chapter 4

The Law of God – The Ten Commandments

Exodus 20:1, 2 (Prologue)

"And God spoke all these words, saying: 'I *am* the Lord your God, who brought you out of the land of Egypt, out of the house of bondage.' "

Luke 10:27

"So he answered and said, 'You shall love the Lord your God with all your heart, with all your soul, with all your strength, and with all your mind,' and 'your neighbor as yourself.' "

***Patriarchs and Prophets*, p. 305**

"Jehovah revealed Himself, not alone in the awful majesty of the judge and lawgiver, but as the compassionate guardian of His people: 'I am the Lord thy God, which have brought thee out of the land of Egypt, out of the house of bondage.' He whom they had already known as their Guide and Deliverer, who had brought them forth from Egypt, making a way for them through the sea, and overthrowing Pharaoh and his hosts, who had thus shown Himself to be above all the gods of Egypt— He it was who now spoke His law.

"The law was not spoken at this time exclusively for the benefit of the Hebrews. God honored them by making them the guardians and keepers of His law, but it was to be held as a sacred trust for the whole world. The precepts of the Decalogue are adapted to all mankind, and they were given for the instruction and government of all. Ten precepts, brief, comprehensive, and authoritative, cover the duty of man to God and to his fellow man; and all based upon the great fundamental principle of love. 'Thou shalt love the Lord thy God with all thy heart, and with all thy soul, and with all thy strength, and with all thy mind; and thy neighbor as thyself.' Luke 10:27. See also Deuteronomy 6:4, 5; Leviticus 19:18. In the Ten Commandments these principles are carried out in detail, and made applicable to the condition and circumstances of man."

"The precepts of the Decalogue are adapted to all mankind, and they were given for the instruction and government of all."

---

*The Law of God -
The Ten Commandments*

Exodus 20:3

"You shall have no other gods before Me."

***Patriarchs and Prophets*, p. 305**

"Jehovah, the eternal, self-existent, uncreated One, Himself the Source and Sustainer of all, is alone entitled to supreme reverence and worship. Man is forbidden to give to any other object the first place in his affections or his service. Whatever we cherish that tends to lessen our love for God or to interfere with the service due Him, of that do we make a god."

Exodus 20:4–6

"You shall not make for yourself a carved image—any likeness *of anything* that *is* in heaven above, or that *is* in the earth beneath, or that *is* in the water under the earth; you shall not bow down to them nor serve them. For I, the Lord your God, *am* a jealous God, visiting the iniquity of the fathers upon the children to the third and fourth *generations* of those who hate Me, but showing mercy to thousands, to those who love Me and keep My commandments."

Patriarchs and Prophets, p. 306

"The second commandment forbids the worship of the true God by images or similitudes. Many heathen nations claimed that their images were mere figures or symbols by which the Deity was worshiped, but God has declared such worship to be sin. The attempt to represent the Eternal One by material objects would lower man's conception of God. The mind, turned away from the infinite perfection of Jehovah, would be attracted to the creature rather than to the Creator. And as his conceptions of God were lowered, so would man become degraded.

" 'I the Lord thy God am a jealous God.' The close and sacred relation of God to His people is represented under the figure of marriage. Idolatry being spiritual adultery, the displeasure of God against it is fitly called jealousy.

" 'Visiting thc iniquity of the fathers upon the children unto the third and fourth generation of them that hate Me.' It is inevitable that children should suffer from the consequences of parental wrongdoing, but they are not punished for the parents' guilt, except as they participate in their sins. It is usually the case, however, that children walk in the steps of their parents. By inheritance and example

the sons become partakers of the father's sin. Wrong tendencies, perverted appetites, and debased morals, as well as physical disease and degeneracy, are transmitted as a legacy from father to son, to the third and fourth generation. This fearful truth should have a solemn power to restrain men from following a course of sin.

" 'Showing mercy unto thousands of them that love Me, and keep My commandments.' In prohibiting the worship of false gods, the second commandment by implication enjoins the worship of the true God. And to those who are faithful in His service, mercy is promised, not merely to the third and fourth generation as is the wrath threatened against those who hate Him, but to *thousands* of generations."

Exodus 20:7

"You shall not take the name of the Lord your God in vain, for the Lord will not hold *him* guiltless who takes His name in vain."

Psalm 111:9

"He has sent redemption to His people; He has commanded His covenant forever: Holy and awesome *is* His name."

Patriarchs and Prophets, pp. 306, 307

"This commandment not only prohibits false oaths and common swearing, but it forbids us to use the name of God in a light or careless manner, without regard to its awful significance. By the thoughtless mention of God in common conversation, by appeals to Him in trivial matters, and by the frequent and thoughtless repetition of His name, we dishonor Him. 'Holy and reverend is His name.' Psalm 111:9. All should meditate upon His majesty, His purity and holiness, that the heart may be impressed with a sense of His exalted character; and His holy name should be uttered with reverence and solemnity."

Exodus 20:8–11

"Remember the Sabbath day, to keep it holy. Six days you shall labor and do all your work, but the seventh day *is* the Sabbath of the Lord your God. *In it* you shall do no work: you, nor your son, nor your daughter, nor your male servant, nor your female servant, nor your cattle, nor your stranger who *is* within your gates. For *in* six days the Lord made the heavens and the earth, the sea, and all that *is* in them, and rested the seventh day. Therefore the Lord blessed the Sabbath day and hallowed it."

Isaiah 58:13

"If you turn away your foot from the Sabbath, *from* doing your pleasure on My holy day, and call the Sabbath a delight, the holy *day* of the Lord honorable, and shall honor Him, not doing your own ways, nor finding your own pleasure, nor speaking *your own* words."

Patriarchs and Prophets, pp. 307, 308

"The Sabbath is not introduced as a new institution but as having been founded at creation. It is to be remembered and observed as the memorial of the Creator's work. Pointing to God as the Maker of the heavens and the earth, it distinguishes the true God from all false gods. All who keep the seventh day signify by this act that they are worshipers of Jehovah. Thus the Sabbath is the sign of man's allegiance to God as long as there are any upon the earth to serve Him. The fourth commandment is the only one of all the ten in which are found both the name and the title of the Lawgiver. It is the only one that shows by whose authority the law is given. Thus it contains the seal of God, affixed to His law as evidence of its authenticity and binding force.

"God has given men six days wherein to labor, and He requires that their own work be done in the six working days. Acts of necessity and mercy are permitted on the Sabbath, the sick and suffering are at all times to be cared for; but unnecessary labor is to be strictly avoided. 'Turn away thy foot from the Sabbath, from doing thy pleasure on My holy day; and call the Sabbath a delight, the holy of the Lord, honorable; and … honor Him, not doing thine own ways, nor finding thine own pleasure.' Isaiah 58:13. Nor does the prohibition end here. 'Nor speaking thine own words,' says the prophet. Those who discuss business matters or lay plans on the Sabbath are regarded by God as though engaged in the actual transaction of business. To keep the Sabbath holy, we should not even allow our minds to dwell upon things of a worldly character. And the commandment includes all within our gates. The inmates of the house are to lay aside their worldly business during the sacred hours. All should unite to honor God by willing service upon His holy day."

Exodus 31:13

"Speak also to the children of Israel, saying: 'Surely My Sabbaths you shall keep, for it *is* a sign between Me and you throughout your generations, that *you* may know that I *am* the Lord who sanctifies you.' "

Exodus 20:12

"Honor your father and your mother, that your days may be long upon the land which the Lord your God is giving you."

Ephesians 6:2

" 'Honor your father and mother,' which is the first commandment with promise."

Patriarchs and Prophets, p. 308
"Parents are entitled to a degree of love and respect which is due to no other person. God Himself, who has placed upon them a responsibility for the souls committed to their charge, has ordained that during the earlier years of life, parents shall stand in the place of God to their children. And he who rejects the rightful authority of his parents is rejecting the authority of God. The fifth commandment requires children not only to yield respect, submission, and obedience to their parents, but also to give them love and tenderness, to lighten their cares, to guard their reputation, and to succor and comfort them in old age. It also enjoins respect for ministers and rulers and for all others to whom God has delegated authority.

"This, says the apostle, 'is the first commandment with promise.' Ephesians 6:2. To Israel, expecting soon to enter Canaan, it was a pledge to the obedient, of long life in that good land; but it has a wider meaning, including all the Israel of God, and promising eternal life upon the earth when it shall be freed from the curse of sin."

Exodus 20:13
"You shall not murder."

1 John 3:15
"Whoever hates his brother is a murderer, and you know that no murderer has eternal life abiding in him."

Patriarchs and Prophets, p. 308
"All acts of injustice that tend to shorten life; the spirit of hatred and revenge, or the indulgence of any passion that leads to injurious acts toward others, or causes us even to wish them harm (for 'whosoever hateth his brother is a murderer [1 John 3:15]'); a selfish neglect of caring for the needy or suffering; all

self-indulgence or unnecessary deprivation or excessive labor that tends to injure health—all these are, to a greater or less degree, violations of the sixth commandment."

Exodus 20:14
"You shall not commit adultery."

Patriarchs and Prophets, p. 308
"This commandment forbids not only acts of impurity, but sensual thoughts and desires, or any practice that tends to excite them. Purity is demanded not only in the outward life but in the secret intents and emotions of the heart. Christ, who taught the far-reaching obligation of the law of God, declared the evil thought or look to be as truly sin as is the unlawful deed."

Exodus 20:15
"You shall not steal."

Patriarchs and Prophets, p. 309
"Both public and private sins are included in this prohibition. The eighth commandment condemns manstealing and slave dealing, and forbids wars of conquest. It condemns theft and robbery. It demands strict integrity in the minutest details of the affairs of life. It forbids overreaching in trade, and requires the payment of just debts or wages. It declares that every attempt to advantage oneself by the ignorance, weakness, or misfortune of another is registered as fraud in the books of heaven."

Exodus 20:16
"You shall not bear false witness against your neighbor."

Patriarchs and Prophets, p. 309
"False speaking in any matter, every attempt or purpose to deceive our neighbor, is here included. An intention to deceive is what

constitutes falsehood. By a glance of the eye, a motion of the hand, an expression of the countenance, a falsehood may be told as effectually as by words. All intentional overstatement, every hint or insinuation calculated to convey an erroneous or exaggerated impression, even the statement of facts in such a manner as to mislead, is falsehood. This precept forbids every effort to injure our neighbor's reputation by misrepresentation or evil surmising, by slander or tale bearing. Even the intentional suppression of truth, by which injury may result to others, is a violation of the ninth commandment."

Exodus 20:17

"You shall not covet your neighbor's house; you shall not covet your neighbor's wife, nor his male servant, nor his female servant, nor his ox, nor his donkey, nor anything that *is* your neighbor's."

Patriarchs and Prophets, p. 309

"The tenth commandment strikes at the very root of all sins, prohibiting the selfish desire, from which springs the sinful act. He who in obedience to God's law refrains from indulging even a sinful desire for that which belongs to another will not be guilty of an act of wrong toward his fellow creatures."

Summary

Patriarchs and Prophets, p. 309

"Such were the sacred precepts of the Decalogue, spoken amid thunder and flame, and with a wonderful display of the power and majesty of the great Lawgiver. God accompanied the proclamation of His law with exhibitions of His power and glory, that His people might never forget the scene, and that they might be impressed with profound veneration for the Author of the law, the Creator of heaven and earth. He would also show to all men the sacredness, the importance, and the permanence of His law."

Patriarchs and Prophets, p. 310

"The minds of the people, blinded and debased by slavery and heathenism, were not prepared to appreciate fully the far-reaching principles of God's ten precepts. That the obligations of the Decalogue might be more fully understood and enforced, additional precepts were given, illustrating and applying the principles of the Ten Commandments. These laws were called judgments, both because they were framed in infinite wisdom and equity and because the magistrates were to give judgment according to them. Unlike the Ten Commandments, they were delivered privately to Moses, who was to communicate them to the people."

Patriarchs and Prophets, p. 311

"These laws were to be recorded by Moses, and carefully treasured as the foundation of the national law, and, with the ten precepts which they were given to illustrate, the condition of the fulfillment of God's promises to Israel."

The Law of God Defined

The Signs of the Times, **November 30, 1904**

"God's character is revealed in the precepts of His law. This is the reason why Satan wishes this law to be made of none effect. But notwithstanding all his efforts, the law stands forth holy and unchanged. It is a transcript of God's character. It cannot be impeached or altered."

Patriarchs and Prophets, pp. 370, 371

"Though this covenant was made with Adam and renewed to Abraham, it could not be ratified until the death of Christ. It had existed by the promise of God since the first intimation of redemption had been given; it had been accepted by faith; yet when ratified by Christ, it is called a *new* covenant. The law of God was the basis of this covenant, which was simply an arrangement for bringing men again into harmony with the divine will, placing them where they could obey God's law."

Romans 3:20

"Therefore by the deeds of the law no flesh will be justified in His sight, for by the law is the knowledge of sin."

Romans 4:15

"Because the law brings about wrath; for where there is no law *there is* no transgression."

1 John 3:4

"Whoever commits sin also commits lawlessness, and sin is lawlessness."

Psalm 40:8

"I delight to do Your will, O my God, and Your law is within my heart."

The Desire of Ages, p. 329

"The yoke that binds to service is the law of God. The great law of love revealed in Eden, proclaimed upon Sinai, and in the new covenant written in the heart, is that which binds the human worker to the will of God. If we were left to follow our own inclinations, to go just where our will would lead us, we should fall into Satan's ranks and become possessors of his attributes. Therefore God confines us to His will, which is high, and noble, and elevating. He desires that we shall patiently and wisely take up the duties of service. The yoke of service Christ Himself has borne in humanity. He said, 'I delight to do Thy will, O My God: yea, Thy law is within My heart.' Psalm 40:8."

Hebrews 10:16

"This is the covenant that I will make with them after those days, says the Lord: I will put My laws into their hearts, and in their minds I will write them."

1 John 5:3

"For this is the love of God, that we keep His commandments. And His commandments are not burdensome."

1 John 2:4

"He who says, 'I know Him,' and does not keep His commandments, is a liar, and the truth is not in him."

Steps to Christ, pp. 60, 61

"The law of God is an expression of His very nature; it is an embodiment of the great principle of love, and hence is the foundation of His government in heaven and earth. If our hearts are renewed in the likeness of God, if the divine love is implanted in the soul, will not the law of God be carried out in the life? When the principle of love is implanted in the heart, when man is renewed after the image of Him that created him, the new-covenant promise is fulfilled, 'I will put My laws into their hearts, and in their minds will I write them.' Hebrews 10:16. And if the law is written in the heart, will it not shape the life? Obedience—the service and allegiance of love—is the true sign of discipleship. Thus the Scripture says, 'This is the love of God, that we keep His commandments.' 'He that saith, I know Him, and keepeth not His commandments, is a liar, and the

Summary of the Mutual Characteristics of God and His Law

God's Law	Characteristic	God
Romans 7:12	Good	Matthew 19:17
Romans 7:12	Just	Deuteronomy 32:4
Romans 7:12	Holy	Leviticus 11:44
Romans 7:14	Spiritual	John 4:23, 24; 2 Corinthians 3:17, 18
Psalm 19:7	Perfect	Deuteronomy 32:4
Psalm 19:8	Pure	Job 4:17; Proverbs 30:5
Luke 16:17	Eternal	1 Timothy 1:17
Psalm 119:142	True	Romans 3:4; John 7:28; 14:6
Matthew 22:35–39	Love	1 John 4:8–12; John 3:16
James 1:25; 2:12	Liberty	2 Corinthians 3:17

truth is not in him.' 1 John 5:3; 2:4. Instead of releasing man from obedience, it is faith, and faith only, that makes us partakers of the grace of Christ, which enables us to render obedience."

The Law of God and the New Covenant

Proverbs 29:18
"Where *there is* no revelation, the people cast off restraint; but happy *is* he who keeps the law."

Deuteronomy 5:29–33
"Oh, that they had such a heart in them that they would fear Me and always keep all My commandments, that it might be well with them and with their children forever.... You shall walk in all the ways which the Lord your God has commanded you, that you may live and *that it may be* well with you, and *that* you may prolong *your* days in the land which you shall possess."

James 2:10
"For whoever shall keep the whole law, and yet stumble in one *point*, he is guilty of all."

Matthew 22:29
"Jesus answered and said to them, 'You are mistaken, not knowing the Scriptures nor the power of God.' "

Luke 24:44, 45
"Then He said to them, 'These *are* the words which I spoke to you while I was still with you, that all things must be fulfilled which were written in the Law of Moses and *the* Prophets and *the* Psalms concerning Me.' And He opened their understanding, that they might comprehend the Scriptures."

The Review and Herald, February 4, 1890

"We have only glimmering light in regard to the exceeding breadth of the law of God. The law spoken from Sinai is a transcript of God's character. Many who claim to be teachers of the truth have no conception of what they are handling when they are presenting the law to the people, because they have not studied it; they have not put their mental powers to the task of understanding its significance. Their God-given powers are diverted and misapplied, and they come far short of apprehending what is truth. They have a smattering of knowledge, but they do not understand the relation of Christ to the law, and cannot present it in such a way as to unfold the plan of salvation to their hearers; for they do not let Christ into their hearts, or bring him into their discourses. They do not feel in their souls that they must plow deeper in their search for truth, so that they may declare the whole counsel of God.

"Christ's relation to the law is but faintly understood, but ignorance will not excuse any man for acting contrary to the principles of the law and the gospel. Many of those who claim to believe the testing truths for these last days, act as though God took no note of their disrespect of, and manifest disobedience to, the principles of his holy law. The law is the expression of his will, and it is through obedience to that law that God proposes to accept the children of men as his sons and daughters. The consequences of transgression reach into eternity, and none of us can afford to be novices in regard to the deep mysteries of salvation. We should understand the relation of Christ to the moral law.

"Our righteousness is found in obedience to God's law through the merits of Jesus Christ. We cannot afford to offend in one point; for if we do, we are pronounced guilty of all [James 2:10]; that is, we are recorded in heaven as transgressors, as disobedient children, unthankful, unholy, who choose the depravity of Satan rather than the purity of Christ. An infinite sacrifice has been made that the moral image of God may be restored to man, through willing obedience to all the commandments of God. Exceeding great is our salvation, for ample provision has been made through the righteousness of Christ, that we may be pure, entire, wanting nothing.

"The plan of salvation opens before the repenting, believing sinner prospects for eternity which the greatest stretch of his imagination cannot compass. If man will keep God's law through faith in Christ, the treasures of heaven will be at his disposal; but the opposite of this will be the result if we refuse to obey God. Man cannot possibly meet the demands of the law of God in human strength alone. His offerings, his works, will all be tainted with sin....

"In the study of the Scriptures there is large scope for the employment of every faculty that God has given us. We should dwell on the law and the gospel, showing the relation of Christ to the great standard of righteousness. The mediatorial work of Christ, the grand and holy mysteries of redemption, are not studied or comprehended by the people who claim to have light in advance of every other people on the face of the earth. Were Jesus personally upon earth, he would address a large number who claim to believe present truth, with the words he addressed to the Pharisees: 'Ye do err, not knowing the Scriptures, nor the power of God [Matthew 22:29].' The most learned of the Jewish scribes did not discern the relation of Christ to the law; they did not comprehend the salvation which was offered. They could not discern the moral excellency of the law at that day, and many today do not understand the Scriptures or the power of God. In the time of Christ the senses of his hearers were clouded by their own teachings and opinions. They mingled their own preconceived notions with the teachings of Christ, and thus were hindered from comprehending the elevated truths he presented. They were blinded to the correct interpretation of the Old Testament Scriptures, but he opened to his disciples their significance, revealing the spiritual and practical bearing of God's commands on life and character. He promised his disciples that after his ascension to his Father, he would send the Holy Spirit, who should bring all things to their remembrance. Jesus had left truths in their possession the value of which they did not comprehend. After his resurrection they were astonished at the words he uttered; but he said unto them, 'These are the words which I spake unto you, while I was yet with you, that all things must be fulfilled, which were written in the law of Moses, and in the prophets, and in the psalms, concerning me. Then opened he their understanding, that they might understand the Scriptures [Luke 24:44, 45].' The disciples were slow of heart to believe all that the Scriptures testified of Christ.

"As long as we are content with our limited knowledge, we are disqualified to obtain rich views of truth. We cannot comprehend the facts connected with the atonement, and the high and holy character of God's law."

The Law of God – The Sabbath

Isaiah 58:13, 14

"If you turn away your foot from the Sabbath, *from* doing your pleasure on My holy day, and call the Sabbath a delight, the holy *day* of the Lord honorable, and shall honor Him, not doing your own ways, nor finding your own pleasure, nor speaking *your own* words, then

you shall delight yourself in the Lord; and I will cause you to ride on the high hills of the earth, and feed you with the heritage of Jacob your father. The mouth of the Lord has spoken."

Isaiah 56:2–7

"Blessed is the man *who* does this, and the son of man *who* lays hold on it; who keeps from defiling the Sabbath, and keeps his hand from doing any evil.

"Do not let the son of the foreigner who has joined himself to the Lord speak, saying, 'The Lord has utterly separated me from His people'; nor let the eunuch say, 'Here I am, a dry tree.' For thus says the Lord: 'To the eunuchs who keep My Sabbaths, and choose what pleases Me, and hold fast My covenant, even to them I will give in My house and within My walls a place and a name better than that of sons and daughters; I will give them an everlasting name that shall not be cut off.

" 'Also the sons of the foreigner who join themselves to the Lord, to serve Him, and to love the name of the Lord, to be His servants—everyone who keeps from defiling the Sabbath, and holds fast My covenant—even them I will bring to My holy mountain, and make them joyful in My house of prayer. Their burnt offerings and their sacrifices *will be* accepted on My altar; for My house shall be called a house of prayer for all nations.' "

Ezekiel 20:11, 12

"And I gave them My statutes and showed them My judgments, 'which, *if* a man does, he shall live by them.' Moreover I also gave them My Sabbaths, to be a sign between them and Me, that they might know that I *am* the Lord who sanctifies them."

Mark 2:27

"And He said to them, 'The Sabbath was made for man, and not man for the Sabbath.' "

Matthew 5:18

"For assuredly, I say to you, till heaven and earth pass away, one jot or one tittle will by no means pass from the law till all is fulfilled."

Isaiah 66:23

" 'And it shall come to pass *that* from one New Moon to another, and from one Sabbath to another, all flesh shall come to worship before Me,' says the Lord."

The Desire of Ages, **p. 283**

"The Sabbath was not for Israel merely, but for the world. It had been made known to man in Eden, and, like the other precepts of the Decalogue, it is of imperishable obligation. Of that law of which the fourth commandment forms a part, Christ declares, 'Till heaven and earth pass, one jot or one tittle shall in nowise pass from the law.' So long as the heavens and the earth endure, the Sabbath will continue as a sign of the Creator's power. And when Eden shall bloom on earth again, God's holy rest day will be honored by all beneath the sun. 'From one Sabbath to another' the inhabitants of the glorified new earth shall go up 'to worship before Me, saith the Lord.' Matthew 5:18; Isaiah 66:23."

Exodus 31:12–18

"And the Lord spoke to Moses, saying, 'Speak also to the children of Israel, saying: "Surely My Sabbaths you shall keep, for it *is* a sign between Me and you throughout your generations, that *you* may know that I *am* the Lord who sanctifies you. You shall keep the Sabbath, therefore, for *it is* holy to you. Everyone who profanes it shall surely be put to death; for whoever does *any* work on it, that person shall be cut off from among his people. Work shall be done for six days, but the seventh *is* the Sabbath of rest, holy to the Lord. Whoever does *any* work on the Sabbath day, he shall surely be put to death. Therefore the children of Israel shall keep the Sabbath, to observe the Sabbath throughout their generations *as* a perpetual covenant. It *is* a sign between Me and the children of Israel forever; for *in* six days the Lord made the heavens and the earth, and on the seventh day He rested and was refreshed." '

"And when He had made an end of speaking with him on Mount Sinai, He gave Moses two tablets of the Testimony, tablets of stone, written with the finger of God."

> "The Sabbath is a sign of the relationship existing between God and His people, a sign that they honor His law. It distinguishes between His loyal subjects and transgressors."

Testimonies for the Church, **Vol. 6, pp. 349, 350**

"When the Lord delivered His people Israel from Egypt and committed to them His law, He taught them that by the observance of the Sabbath they were to be distinguished from idolaters. It was this that made the distinction between those who acknowledge the sovereignty of God and those who refuse to accept Him as their Creator and King. 'It is a sign between Me and the children of Israel forever,' the Lord said. 'Wherefore the children of Israel shall keep the Sabbath, to observe the Sabbath throughout their generations, for a perpetual covenant.' Exodus 31:17, 16.

"As the Sabbath was the sign that distinguished Israel when they came out of Egypt to enter the earthly Canaan, so it is the sign that now distinguishes God's people as they come out from the world to enter the heavenly rest. The Sabbath is a sign of the relationship existing between God and His people, a sign that they honor His law. It distinguishes between His loyal subjects and transgressors.

"From the pillar of cloud Christ declared concerning the Sabbath: 'Verily My Sabbaths ye shall keep: for it is a sign between Me and you throughout your generations; that ye may know that I am the Lord that doth sanctify you.' Exodus 31:13. The Sabbath given to the world as the sign of God as the Creator is also the sign of Him as the Sanctifier. The power that created all things is the power that re-creates the soul in His own likeness. To those who keep holy the Sabbath day it is the sign of sanctification. True sanctification is harmony with God, oneness with Him in character. It is received through obedience to those principles that are the transcript of His character. And the Sabbath is the sign of obedience. He who from the heart obeys the fourth commandment will obey the whole law. He is sanctified through obedience.

"To us as to Israel the Sabbath is given 'for a perpetual covenant [Exodus 31:16].' To those who reverence His holy day the Sabbath is a sign that God recognizes them as His chosen people. It is a pledge that He will fulfill to them His covenant. Every soul who accepts the sign of God's government places himself under the divine, everlasting covenant. He fastens himself to the golden chain of obedience, every link of which is a promise."

> ## "The Sabbath given to the world as the sign of God as the Creator is also the sign of Him as the Sanctifier."

***Patriarchs and Prophets*, pp. 47, 48**

"The great Jehovah had laid the foundations of the earth; He had dressed the whole world in the garb of beauty and had filled it with things useful to man; He had created all the wonders of the land and of the sea. In six days the great work of creation had been accomplished. And God 'rested on the seventh day from all His work which He had made. And God blessed the seventh day, and sanctified it: because that in it He had rested from all His work which God created and made.' God looked with satisfaction upon the work of His hands. All was perfect, worthy of its divine Author, and He rested, not as one weary, but as well pleased with the fruits of His wisdom and goodness and the manifestations of His glory.

"After resting upon the seventh day, God sanctified it, or set it apart, as a day of rest for man. Following the example of the Creator, man was to rest upon this sacred day, that as he should look upon the heavens and the earth, he might reflect upon God's great work of creation; and that as he should behold the evidences of God's wisdom and goodness, his heart might be filled with love and reverence for his Maker.

"In Eden, God set up the memorial of His work of creation, in placing His blessing upon the seventh day. The Sabbath was committed to Adam, the father and representative of the whole human family. Its observance was to be an act of grateful acknowledgment, on the part of all who should dwell upon the earth, that God was their Creator and their rightful Sovereign; that they were the work of His hands and the subjects of His authority. Thus the institution was wholly commemorative, and given to all mankind. There was nothing in it shadowy or of restricted application to any people."

The Great Controversy, p. 434, 435

"In the very bosom of the Decalogue is the fourth commandment, as it was first proclaimed: 'Remember the Sabbath day, to keep it holy. Six days shalt thou labor, and do all thy work: but the seventh day is the Sabbath of the Lord thy God: in it thou shalt not do any work, thou, nor thy son, nor thy daughter, thy manservant, nor thy maidservant, nor thy cattle, nor thy stranger that is within thy gates: for in six days the Lord made heaven and earth, the sea, and all that in them is, and rested the seventh day: wherefore the Lord blessed the Sabbath day, and hallowed it.' Exodus 20:8–11.

"The Spirit of God impressed the hearts of those students of His word. The conviction was urged upon them that they had ignorantly transgressed this precept by disregarding the Creator's rest day. They began to examine the reasons for observing the first day of the week instead of the day which God had sanctified. They could find no evidence in the Scriptures that the fourth commandment had been abolished, or that the Sabbath had been changed; the blessing which first hallowed the seventh day had never been removed. They had been honestly seeking to know and to do God's will; now, as they saw themselves transgressors of His law, sorrow filled their hearts, and they manifested their loyalty to God by keeping His Sabbath holy."

Ezekiel 20:20

"Hallow My Sabbaths, and they will be a sign between Me and you, that you may know that I *am* the Lord your God."

Revelation 14:7

"Saying with a loud voice, 'Fear God and give glory to Him, for the hour of His judgment has come; and worship Him who made heaven and earth, the sea and springs of water.' "

Genesis 2:2, 3

"And on the seventh day God ended His work which He had done, and He rested on the seventh day from all His work which He had done. Then God blessed the seventh day and sanctified it, because in it He rested from all His work which God had created and made."

The Great Controversy, pp. 437, 438

"In Revelation 14, men are called upon to worship the Creator; and the prophecy brings to view a class that, as the result of the threefold message, are keeping the commandments of God. One of these commandments points directly to God as the Creator. The fourth precept declares: 'The seventh day is the Sabbath of the Lord thy God: ... for in six days the Lord made heaven and earth, the sea, and all that in them is, and rested the seventh day: wherefore the Lord blessed the Sabbath day, and hallowed it.' Exodus 20:10, 11. Concerning the Sabbath, the Lord says, further, that it is 'a sign, ... that ye may know that I am the Lord your God.' Ezekiel 20:20. And the reason given is: 'For in six days the Lord made heaven and earth, and on the seventh day He rested, and was refreshed.' Exodus 31:17.

" 'The importance of the Sabbath as the memorial of creation is that it keeps ever present the true reason why worship is due to

God'—because He is the Creator, and we are His creatures. 'The Sabbath therefore lies at the very foundation of divine worship, for it teaches this great truth in the most impressive manner, and no other institution does this. The true ground of divine worship, not of that on the seventh day merely, but of all worship, is found in the distinction between the Creator and His creatures. This great fact can never become obsolete, and must never be forgotten.'—J. N. Andrews, *History of the Sabbath*, chapter 27. It was to keep this truth ever before the minds of men, that God instituted the Sabbath in Eden [Genesis 2:2, 3]; and so long as the fact that He is our Creator continues to be a reason why we should worship Him, so long the Sabbath will continue as its sign and memorial. Had the Sabbath been universally kept, man's thoughts and affections would have been led to the Creator as the object of reverence and worship, and there would never have been an idolater, an atheist, or an infidel. The keeping of the Sabbath is a sign of loyalty to the true God, 'Him that made heaven, and earth, and the sea, and the fountains of waters [Revelation 14:7].' It follows that the message which commands men to worship God and keep His commandments will especially call upon them to keep the fourth commandment."

Selected Messages, Book 2, p. 55

"God's tried and tested people will find their power in the sign spoken of in Exodus 31:12–18. They are to take their stand on the living Word—'It is written.' This is the only foundation upon which they can stand securely. Those who have broken their covenant with God will in that day be without hope and without God in the world.

"The worshipers of God will be especially distinguished by their regard for the fourth commandment—since this is the sign of His creative power and the witness to His claim upon man's reverence and homage."

The Perpetuity of the Law of God

Psalm 89:34
"My covenant I will not break, nor alter the word that has gone out of My lips."

Psalm 119:152
"Concerning Your testimonies, I have known of old that You have founded them forever."

Deuteronomy 5:22
"These words the Lord spoke to all your assembly, in the mountain from the midst of the fire, the cloud, and the thick darkness, with a loud voice; and He added no more. And He wrote them on two tablets of stone and gave them to me."

Deuteronomy 4:13
"So He declared to you His covenant which He commanded you to perform, the Ten Commandments; and He wrote them on two tablets of stone."

Malachi 3:6
"For I *am* the Lord, I do not change; therefore you are not consumed, O sons of Jacob."

Matthew 24:35; Luke 21:33
"Heaven and earth will pass away, but My words will by no means pass away."

The Story of Redemption, p. 145
"The law of God existed before man was created. The angels were governed by it. Satan fell because he transgressed the principles of God's government. After Adam and Eve were created, God made known to them His law.

It was not then written, but was rehearsed to them by Jehovah."

Early Writings, p. 217
"I was shown that the law of God would stand fast forever, and exist in the new earth to all eternity. At the creation, when the foundations of the earth were laid, the sons of God looked with admiration upon the work of the Creator, and all the heavenly host shouted for joy. It was then that the foundation of the Sabbath was laid. At the close of the six days of creation, God rested on the seventh day from all His work which He had made; and He blessed the seventh day and sanctified it, because that in it He had rested from all His work. The Sabbath was instituted in Eden before the fall, and was observed by Adam and Eve, and all the heavenly host. God rested on the seventh day, and blessed and hallowed it. I saw that the Sabbath never will be done away; but that the redeemed saints, and all the angelic host, will observe it in honor of the great Creator to all eternity."

Matthew 5:17, 18
"Do not think that I came to destroy the Law or the Prophets. I did not come to destroy but to fulfill. For assuredly, I say to you, till heaven and earth pass away, one jot or one tittle will by no means pass from the law till all is fulfilled."

Psalm 119:89
"Forever, O Lord, Your word is settled in heaven."

Psalm 111:7, 8
"The works of His hands *are* verity and justice; all His precepts *are* sure. They stand fast forever and ever, *and are* done in truth and uprightness."

The Great Controversy, p. 434
"The law of God in the sanctuary in heaven is the great original, of which the precepts inscribed upon the tables of stone and recorded by Moses in the Pentateuch were an unerring transcript. Those who arrived at an understanding of this important point were thus led to see the sacred, unchanging character of the divine law. They saw, as never before, the force of the Saviour's words: 'Till heaven and earth pass, one jot or one tittle shall in no wise pass from the law.' Matthew 5:18. The law of God, being a revelation of His will, a transcript of His character, must forever endure, 'as a faithful witness in heaven.' Not one command has been annulled; not a jot or tittle has been changed. Says the psalmist: 'Forever, O Lord, Thy word is settled in heaven.' 'All His commandments are sure. They stand fast for ever and ever.' Psalm 119:89; 111:7, 8."

> **"The law of God is as sacred as God Himself. It is a revelation of His will, a transcript of His character, the expression of divine love and wisdom."**

Patriarchs and Prophets, p. 52
"The law of God is as sacred as God Himself. It is a revelation of His will, a transcript of His character, the expression of divine love and wisdom. The harmony of creation depends upon the perfect conformity of all beings, of everything, animate and inanimate, to the law of the Creator. God has ordained laws for the government, not only of living beings, but of all the operations of nature. Everything is under fixed laws, which cannot be disregarded. But while everything in nature is governed by

natural laws, man alone, of all that inhabits the earth, is amenable to moral law. To man, the crowning work of creation, God has given power to understand His requirements, to comprehend the justice and beneficence of His law, and its sacred claims upon him; and of man unswerving obedience is required."

Isaiah 59:14

"Justice is turned back, and righteousness stands afar off; for truth is fallen in the street, and equity cannot enter."

The Great Controversy, pp. 583–588

"In rejecting the truth, men reject its Author. In trampling upon the law of God, they deny the authority of the Law-giver. It is as easy to make an idol of false doctrines and theories as to fashion an idol of wood or stone. By misrepresenting the attributes of God, Satan leads men to conceive of Him in a false character. With many, a philosophical idol is enthroned in the place of Jehovah; while the living God, as He is revealed in His word, in Christ, and in the works of creation, is worshiped by but few. Thousands deify nature while they deny the God of nature. Though in a different form, idolatry exists in the Christian world today as verily as it existed among ancient Israel in the days of Elijah. The god of many professedly wise men, of philosophers, poets, politicians, journalists—the god of polished fashionable circles, of many colleges and universities, even of some theological institutions—is little better than Baal, the sun-god of Phoenicia.

"No error accepted by the Christian world strikes more boldly against the authority of Heaven, none is more directly opposed to the dictates of reason, none is more pernicious in its results, than the modern doctrine, so rapidly gaining ground, that God's law is no longer binding upon men. Every nation has its laws, which command respect and obedience; no government could exist without them; and can it be conceived that the Creator of the heavens and the earth has no law to govern the beings He has made? Suppose that prominent ministers were publicly to teach that the statutes which govern their land and protect the rights of its citizens were not obligatory—that they restricted the liberties of the people, and therefore ought not to be obeyed; how long would such men be tolerated in the pulpit? But is it a graver offense to disregard the laws of states and nations than to trample upon those divine precepts which are the foundation of all government?

"It would be far more consistent for nations to abolish their statutes, and permit the people to do as they please, than for the Ruler of the universe to annul His law, and leave the world without a standard to condemn the guilty or justify the obedient. Would we know the result of making void the law of God? The experiment has been tried. Terrible were the scenes enacted in France when atheism became the controlling power. It was then demonstrated to the world that to throw off the restraints which God has imposed is to accept the rule of the cruelest of tyrants. When the standard of righteousness is set aside, the way is open for the prince of evil to establish his power in the earth.

"Wherever the divine precepts are rejected, sin ceases to appear sinful or righteousness desirable. Those who refuse to submit to the government of God are wholly unfitted to govern themselves. Through their pernicious teachings the spirit of insubordination is implanted in the hearts of children and youth, who are naturally impatient of control; and a lawless, licentious state of society results. While scoffing at the credulity of those who obey the requirements of God, the multitudes eagerly accept the delusions of Satan. They give the rein to lust and practice the sins which have called down judgments upon the heathen.

"Those who teach the people to regard lightly the commandments of God sow disobedience to reap disobedience. Let the restraint imposed by the divine law be wholly cast aside, and human laws would soon be disregarded. Because God forbids dishonest practices, coveting, lying, and defrauding, men are ready to trample upon His statutes as a hindrance to their worldly prosperity; but the results of banishing these precepts would be such as they do not anticipate. If the law were not binding, why should any fear to transgress? Property would no longer be safe. Men would obtain their neighbor's possessions by violence, and the strongest would become richest. Life itself would not be respected. The marriage vow would no longer stand as a sacred bulwark to protect the family. He who had the power, would, if he desired, take his neighbor's wife by violence. The fifth commandment would be set aside with the fourth. Children would not shrink from taking the life of their parents if by so doing they could obtain the desire of their corrupt hearts. The civilized world would become a horde of robbers and assassins; and peace, rest, and happiness would be banished from the earth.

"Already the doctrine that men are released from obedience to God's requirements has weakened the force of moral obligation and opened the floodgates of iniquity upon the world. Lawlessness, dissipation, and corruption are sweeping in upon us like an overwhelming tide. In the family, Satan is at work. His banner waves, even in professedly Christian households. There is envy, evil surmising, hypocrisy, estrangement, emulation, strife, betrayal of sacred trusts, indulgence of lust. The whole system of religious principles and doctrines, which should form the foundation and framework of social life, seems to be a tottering mass, ready to fall to ruin. The vilest of criminals, when thrown into prison for their offenses, are often made the recipients of gifts and attentions as if they had attained an enviable distinction. Great publicity is given to their character and crimes. The press publishes the revolting details of vice, thus initiating others into the practice of fraud, robbery, and murder; and Satan exults in the success of his hellish schemes. The infatuation of vice, the wanton taking of life, the terrible increase of intemperance and iniquity of every order and degree, should arouse all who fear God, to inquire what can be done to stay the tide of evil.

"Courts of justice are corrupt. Rulers are actuated by desire for gain and love of sensual pleasure. Intemperance has beclouded the faculties of many so that Satan has almost complete control of them. Jurists are perverted, bribed, deluded. Drunkenness and revelry, passion, envy, dishonesty of every sort, are represented among those who administer the laws. 'Justice standeth afar off: for truth is fallen in the street, and equity cannot enter.' Isaiah 59:14.

"The iniquity and spiritual darkness that prevailed under the supremacy of Rome were the inevitable result of her suppression of the Scriptures; but where is to be found the cause of the widespread infidelity, the rejection of the law of God, and the consequent corruption, under the full blaze of gospel light in an age of religious freedom? Now that Satan can no longer keep the world under his control by withholding the Scriptures, he resorts to other means to accomplish the same object. To destroy faith in the Bible serves his purpose as well as to destroy the Bible itself. By introducing the belief that God's law is not binding, he as effectually leads men to transgress as if they were wholly ignorant of its precepts. And now, as in former ages, he has worked through the church to further his designs. The religious organizations of the day have refused to listen to unpopular truths plainly brought to view in the Scriptures, and in combating them they have adopted interpretations and taken positions which have sown broadcast the seeds of skepticism. Clinging to the papal error of natural immortality and man's consciousness in death, they have rejected the only defense against the delusions of spiritualism. The doctrine of eternal torment has led many to disbelieve the Bible. And as the claims of the fourth commandment are urged upon the people, it is found that the observance of the seventh-day Sabbath is enjoined; and as the only way to free themselves from a duty which they are unwilling to perform, many popular teachers declare that the law of God is no longer binding. Thus they cast away the law and the Sabbath together. As the work of Sabbath reform extends, this rejection of the divine law to avoid the claims of the fourth commandment will become well-nigh universal. The teachings of religious leaders have opened the door to infidelity, to spiritualism, and to contempt for God's holy law; and upon these leaders rests a fearful responsibility for the iniquity that exists in the Christian world.

"Yet this very class put forth the claim that the fast-spreading corruption is largely attributable to the desecration of the so-called 'Christian sabbath,' and that the enforcement of Sunday observance would greatly improve the morals of society. This claim is especially urged in America, where the doctrine of the true Sabbath has been most widely preached. Here the temperance work, one of the most prominent and important of moral reforms, is often combined with the Sunday movement, and the advocates of the latter represent themselves as laboring to promote the highest interest of society; and those who refuse to unite with them are denounced as the enemies of temperance and reform. But the fact that a movement to establish error is connected with a work which is in itself good, is not an argument in favor of the error. We may disguise poison by mingling it with wholesome food, but we do not change its nature. On the contrary, it is rendered more dangerous, as it is more likely to be taken unawares. It is one of Satan's devices to combine with falsehood just enough truth to give it plausibility. The leaders of the Sunday movement may advocate reforms which the people need, principles which are in harmony with the Bible; yet while there is with these a requirement which is contrary to God's law, His servants cannot unite with them. Nothing can justify them in setting aside the commandments of God for the precepts of men."

The Law of God – The Standard in the Judgment

Revelation 14:7, 12
"Saying with a loud voice, 'Fear God and give glory to Him, for the hour of His judgment has come; and worship Him who made heaven and earth, the sea and springs of water.' "

"Here is the patience of the saints; here *are* those who keep the commandments of God and the faith of Jesus."

Romans 2:12–16
"For as many as have sinned without law will also perish without law, and as many as have sinned in the law will be judged by the law (for not the hearers of the law *are* just in the sight of God, but the doers of the law will be

justified; for when Gentiles, who do not have the law, by nature do the things in the law, these, although not having the law, are a law to themselves, who show the work of the law written in their hearts, their conscience also bearing witness, and between themselves *their* thoughts accusing or else excusing *them*) in the day when God will judge the secrets of men by Jesus Christ, according to my gospel."

Hebrews 11:6
"But without faith *it is* impossible to please *Him*, for he who comes to God must believe that He is, and *that* He is a rewarder of those who diligently seek Him."

Romans 14:23
"But he who doubts is condemned if he eats, because *he does* not *eat* from faith; for whatever *is* not from faith is sin."

Ecclesiastes 12:13
"Let us hear the conclusion of the whole matter: fear God and keep His commandments, for this is man's all."

1 John 5:3
"For this is the love of God, that we keep His commandments. And His commandments are not burdensome."

Proverbs 28:9
"One who turns away his ear from hearing the law, even his prayer *is* an abomination."

***The Great Controversy*, pp. 435, 436**
" 'The hour of His judgment is come,' points to the closing work of Christ's ministration for the salvation of men. It heralds a truth which must be proclaimed until the Saviour's intercession shall cease and He shall return to the earth to take His people to Himself. The work

of judgment which began in 1844 must continue until the cases of all are decided, both of the living and the dead; hence it will extend to the close of human probation. That men may be prepared to stand in the judgment, the message commands them to 'fear God, and give glory to Him,' 'and worship Him that made heaven, and earth, and the sea, and the fountains of waters.' The result of an acceptance of these messages is given in the word: 'Here are they that keep the commandments of God, and the faith of Jesus.' In order to be prepared for the judgment, it is necessary that men should keep the law of God. That law will be the standard of character in the judgment. The apostle Paul declares: 'As many as have sinned in the law shall be judged by the law, … in the day when God shall judge the secrets of men by Jesus Christ.' And he says that 'the doers of the law shall be justified.' Romans 2:12–16. Faith is essential in order to the keeping of the law of God; for 'without faith it is impossible to please Him.' And 'whatsoever is not of faith is sin.' Hebrews 11:6; Romans 14:23.

"By the first angel, men are called upon to 'fear God, and give glory to Him' and to worship Him as the Creator of the heavens and the earth. In order to do this, they must obey His law. Says the wise man: 'Fear God, and keep His commandments: for this is the whole duty of man.' Ecclesiastes 12:13. Without obedience to His commandments no worship can be pleasing to God. 'This is the love of God, that we keep His commandments.' 'He that turneth away his ear from hearing the law, even his prayer shall be abomination.' 1 John 5:3; Proverbs 28:9."

James 2:10–12
"For whoever shall keep the whole law, and yet stumble in one *point*, he is guilty of all. For

He who said, 'Do not commit adultery,' also said, 'Do not murder.' Now if you do not commit adultery, but you do murder, you have become a transgressor of the law. So speak and so do as those who will be judged by the law of liberty."

"In the beginning was the Word, and the Word was with God, and the Word was God. He was in the beginning with God. All things were made through Him, and without Him nothing was made that was made."
John 1:1–3

"The Bible recognizes no long ages in which the earth was slowly evolved from chaos. Of each successive day of creation, the sacred record declares that it consisted of the evening and the morning, like all other days that have followed."
Patriarchs and Prophets, p. 112

Chapter 5

The Creation

Psalm 33:6–9

"By the word of the Lord the heavens were made, and all the host of them by the breath of His mouth.… For He spoke, and it was *done*; He commanded, and it stood fast."

Genesis 1:1–31

"In the beginning God created the heavens and the earth. The earth was without form, and void; and darkness *was* on the face of the deep. And the Spirit of God was hovering over the face of the waters.

"Then God said, 'Let there be light'; and there was light. And God saw the light, that *it was* good; and God divided the light from the darkness. God called the light Day, and the darkness He called Night. So the evening and the morning were the first day.

"Then God said, 'Let there be a firmament in the midst of the waters, and let it divide the waters from the waters.' Thus God made the firmament, and divided the waters which *were* under the firmament from the waters which *were* above the firmament; and it was so. And God called the firmament Heaven. So the evening and the morning were the second day.

"Then God said, 'Let the waters under the heavens be gathered together into one place, and let the dry *land* appear'; and it was so. And God called the dry *land* Earth, and the gathering together of the waters He called Seas. And God saw that *it was* good.

"Then God said, 'Let the earth bring forth grass, the herb *that* yields seed, *and* the fruit tree *that* yields fruit according to its kind, whose seed is in itself, on the earth'; and it was so. And the earth brought forth grass, the herb *that* yields seed according to its kind, and the tree *that* yields fruit, whose seed *is* in itself according to its kind. And God saw that *it was* good. So the evening and the morning were the third day.

"Then God said, 'Let there be lights in the firmament of the heavens to divide the day from the night; and let them be for signs and seasons, and for days and years; and let them be for lights in the firmament of the heavens to give light on the earth'; and it was so. Then God made two great lights: the greater light to rule the day, and the lesser light to rule the night. *He made* the stars also. God set them in the firmament of the heavens to give light on the earth, and to rule over the day and over the night, and to divide the light from the darkness. And God saw that *it was* good. So the evening and the morning were the fourth day.

"Then God said, 'Let the waters abound with an abundance of living creatures, and let birds fly above the earth across the face of the firmament of the heavens.' So God created great sea creatures and every living thing that moves, with which the waters abounded, according to their kind, and every winged bird according to its kind. And God saw that *it was* good. And God blessed them, saying, 'Be fruitful and multiply, and fill the waters in the seas, and let birds multiply on the earth.' So the evening and the morning were the fifth day.

"Then God said, 'Let the earth bring forth the living creature according to its kind: cattle and creeping thing and beast of the earth, *each* according to its kind'; and it was so. And God made the beast of the earth according to its kind, cattle according to its kind, and everything that creeps on the earth according to its kind. And God saw that *it was* good.

"Then God said, 'Let Us make man in Our image, according to Our likeness; let them have dominion over the fish of the sea, over the birds of the air, and over the cattle, over all the earth and over every creeping thing that creeps on the earth.' So God created man in His *own* image; in the image of God He created him; male and female He created them. Then God blessed them, and God said to them, 'Be fruitful and multiply; fill the earth and subdue it; have dominion over the fish of the sea, over the birds of the air, and over every living thing that moves on the earth.'

"And God said, 'See, I have given you every herb *that* yields seed which *is* on the face of all the earth, and every tree whose fruit yields seed; to you it shall be for food. Also, to every beast of the earth, to every bird of the air, and to everything that creeps on the earth, in which *there is* life, *I have given* every green herb for food'; and it was so. Then God saw everything that He had made, and indeed *it was* very good. So the evening and the morning were the sixth day."

Genesis 2:1–3

"Thus the heavens and the earth, and all the host of them, were finished. And on the seventh day God ended His work which He had done, and He rested on the seventh day from all His work which He had done. Then God blessed the seventh day and sanctified it, because in it He rested from all His work which God had created and made."

Genesis 2:4–25

"This *is* the history of the heavens and the earth when they were created, in the day that the Lord God made the earth and the heavens, before any plant of the field was in the earth and before any herb of the field had grown. For the Lord God had not caused it to rain on the earth, and *there was* no man to till the ground; but a mist went up from the earth and watered the whole face of the ground.

"And the Lord God formed man *of* the dust of the ground, and breathed into his nostrils the breath of life; and man became a living being.

"The Lord God planted a garden eastward in Eden, and there He put the man whom He had formed. And out of the ground the Lord God made every tree grow that is pleasant to the sight and good for food. The tree of life *was* also in the midst of the garden, and the tree of the knowledge of good and evil.

"Now a river went out of Eden to water the garden, and from there it parted and became four riverheads. The name of the first *is* Pishon; it *is* the one which skirts the whole land of Havilah, where *there is* gold. And the gold of that land *is* good. Bdellium and the onyx stone *are* there. The name of the second river *is* Gihon; it *is* the one which goes around the whole land of Cush. The name of the third river *is* Hiddekel; it *is* the one which goes toward the east of Assyria. The fourth river *is* the Euphrates.

"Then the Lord God took the man and put him in the garden of Eden to tend and keep it. And the Lord God commanded the man, saying, 'Of every tree of the garden you may freely eat; but of the tree of the knowledge of good and evil you shall not eat, for in the day that you eat of it you shall surely die.'

"And the Lord God said, '*It is* not good that man should be alone; I will make him a helper comparable to him.' Out of the ground the Lord God formed every beast of the field and every bird of the air, and brought *them* to Adam to see what he would call them. And whatever Adam called each living creature, that *was* its name. So Adam gave names to all cattle, to the birds of the air, and to every beast of the field. But for Adam there was not found a helper comparable to him.

"And the Lord God caused a deep sleep to fall on Adam, and he slept; and He took one of his ribs, and closed up the flesh in its place. Then the rib which the Lord God had taken from man He made into a woman, and He brought her to the man.

"And Adam said: 'This *is* now bone of my bones and flesh of my flesh; she shall be called Woman, because she was taken out of Man.'

"Therefore a man shall leave his father and mother and be joined to his wife, and they shall become one flesh.

"And they were both naked, the man and his wife, and were not ashamed."

Patriarchs and Prophets, p. 46
"God Himself gave Adam a companion. He provided 'an help meet for him'—a helper corresponding to him—one who was fitted to be his companion, and who could be one with him in love and sympathy. Eve was created from a rib taken from the side of Adam, signifying that she was not to control him as the head, nor to be trampled under his feet as an inferior, but to stand by his side as an equal, to be loved and protected by him. A part of man, bone of his bone, and flesh of his flesh, she was his second self, showing the close union and the affectionate attachment that should exist in this relation. 'For no man ever yet hated his own flesh; but nourisheth and cherisheth it.' Ephesians 5:29. 'Therefore shall a man leave his father and his mother, and shall cleave unto his wife; and they shall be one.' "

Patriarchs and Prophets, p. 111
"Like the Sabbath, the week originated at creation, and it has been preserved and brought down to us through Bible history. God Himself measured off the first week as a sample for successive weeks to the close of time. Like every other, it consisted of seven literal days. Six days were employed in the work of creation; upon the seventh, God rested, and He then blessed this day and set it apart as a day of rest for man."

Patriarchs and Prophets, p. 112
" 'By the word of the Lord were the heavens made; and all the host of them by the breath of His mouth.' 'For He spake, and it was done; He commanded, and it stood fast.' Psalm 33:6, 9. The Bible recognizes no long ages in which the earth was slowly evolved from chaos. Of each successive day of creation, the sacred record declares that it consisted of the evening and the morning, like all other days that have followed. At the close of each day is given the result of the Creator's work. The statement is made at the close of the first week's record, 'These are the generations of the heavens and of the earth when they were created.' Genesis 2:4. But this does not convey the idea that the days of creation were other than literal days. Each day was called a generation, because that in it God generated, or produced, some new portion of His work."

Hebrews 11:3
"By faith we understand that the worlds were framed by the word of God, so that the things which are seen were not made of things which are visible."

Hebrews 1:1, 2

"God, who at various times and in various ways spoke in time past to the fathers by the prophets, has in these last days spoken to us by *His* Son, whom He has appointed heir of all things, through whom also He made the worlds."

John 1:1–3

"In the beginning was the Word, and the Word was with God, and the Word was God. He was in the beginning with God. All things were made through Him, and without Him nothing was made that was made."

Revelation 4:11

"You are worthy, O Lord, to receive glory and honor and power; for You created all things, and by Your will they exist and were created."

Revelation 14:6, 7

"Then I saw another angel flying in the midst of heaven, having the everlasting gospel to preach to those who dwell on the earth—to every nation, tribe, tongue, and people—saying with a loud voice, 'Fear God and give glory to Him, for the hour of His judgment has come; and worship Him who made heaven and earth, the sea and springs of water.' "

Isaiah 40:26

"Lift up your eyes on high, and see who has created these *things*, Who brings out their host by number; He calls them all by name, by the greatness of His might and the strength of *His* power; not one is missing."

Isaiah 42:5

"Thus says God the Lord, Who created the heavens and stretched them out, Who spread forth the earth and that which comes from it, Who gives breath to the people on it, and spirit to those who walk on it."

Isaiah 45:8, 12, 18

"Rain down, you heavens, from above, and let the skies pour down righteousness; let the earth open, let them bring forth salvation, and let righteousness spring up together. I, the Lord, have created it."

"I have made the earth, and created man on it. I—My hands—stretched out the heavens, and all their host I have commanded."

"For thus says the Lord, Who created the heavens, Who is God, Who formed the earth and made it, Who has established it, Who did not create it in vain, Who formed it to be inhabited: 'I *am* the Lord, and *there is* no other.' "

Colossians 1:16

"For by Him all things were created that are in heaven and that are on earth, visible and invisible, whether thrones or dominions or principalities or powers. All things were created through Him and for Him."

Exodus 20:8–11

"Remember the Sabbath day, to keep it holy. Six days you shall labor and do all your work, but the seventh day *is* the Sabbath of the Lord your God. *In it* you shall do no work: you, nor your son, nor your daughter, nor your male servant, nor your female servant, nor your cattle, nor your stranger who *is* within your gates. For *in* six days the Lord made the heavens and the earth, the sea, and all that *is* in them, and rested the seventh day. Therefore the Lord blessed the Sabbath day and hallowed it."

Psalm 104:5

"*You who* laid the foundations of the earth, so *that* it should not be moved forever."

Psalm 8:6–8

"You have made him to have dominion over the works of Your hands; You have put all *things* under his feet, all sheep and oxen— even the beasts of the field, the birds of the air, and the fish of the sea that pass through the paths of the seas."

***Patriarchs and Prophets*, p. 44, 45**

" 'By the word of the Lord were the heavens made; and all the host of them by the breath of His mouth.' 'For He spake, and it was;' 'He commanded, and it stood fast.' Psalm 33:6, 9. He 'laid the foundations of the earth, that it should not be removed forever.' Psalm 104:5.

"As the earth came forth from the hand of its Maker, it was exceedingly beautiful. Its surface was diversified with mountains, hills, and plains, interspersed with noble rivers and lovely lakes; but the hills and mountains were not abrupt and rugged, abounding in terrific steeps and frightful chasms, as they now do; the sharp, ragged edges of earth's rocky framework were buried beneath the fruitful soil, which everywhere produced a luxuriant growth of verdure. There were no loathsome swamps or barren deserts. Graceful shrubs and delicate flowers greeted the eye at every turn. The heights were crowned with trees more majestic than any that now exist. The air, untainted by foul miasma, was clear and healthful. The entire landscape outvied in beauty the decorated grounds of the proudest palace. The angelic host viewed the scene with delight, and rejoiced at the wonderful works of God.

"After the earth with its teeming animal and vegetable life had been called into existence, man, the crowning work of the Creator, and the one for whom the beautiful earth had been fitted up, was brought upon the stage of action. To him was given dominion over all that his eye could behold; for 'God said, Let Us make man in Our image, after Our likeness: and let them have dominion over ... all the earth.... So God created man in His own image; ... male and female created He them.' Here is clearly set forth the origin of the human race; and the divine record is so plainly stated that there is no occasion for erroneous conclusions. God created man in His own image. Here is no mystery. There is no ground for the supposition that man was evolved by slow degrees of development from the lower forms of animal or vegetable life. Such teaching lowers the great work of the Creator to the level of man's narrow, earthly conceptions. Men are so intent upon excluding God from the sovereignty of the universe that they degrade man and defraud him of the dignity of his origin. He who set the starry worlds on high and tinted with delicate skill the flowers of the field, who filled the earth and the heavens with the wonders of His power, when He came to crown His glorious work, to place one in the midst to stand as ruler of the fair earth, did not fail to create a being worthy of the hand that gave him life. The genealogy of our race, as given by inspiration, traces back its origin, not to a line of developing germs, mollusks, and quadrupeds, but to the great Creator. Though formed from the dust, Adam was 'the son of God.'

" 'For He spake, and it was;' 'He commanded, and it stood fast.' Psalm 33:6, 9. He 'laid the foundations of the earth, that it should not be removed forever.' Psalm 104:5."

"He was placed, as God's representative, over the lower orders of being. They cannot understand or acknowledge the sovereignty of God, yet they were made capable of loving and serving man. The psalmist says, 'Thou madest him to have dominion over the works of Thy hands; Thou hast put all things under his feet: … the beasts of the field; the fowl of the air, … and whatsoever passeth through the paths of the seas.' Psalm 8:6–8."

Patriarchs and Prophets, **p. 52**

"But while everything in nature is governed by natural laws, man alone, of all that inhabits the earth, is amenable to moral law. To man, the crowning work of creation, God has given power to understand His requirements, to comprehend the justice and beneficence of His law, and its sacred claims upon him; and of man unswerving obedience is required."

Psalm 65:6

"Who established the mountains by His strength, *being* clothed with power."

Psalm 95:5

"The sea *is* His, for He made it; and His hands formed the dry *land*."

The Desire of Ages, **p. 20**

"In the beginning, God was revealed in all the works of creation. It was Christ that spread the heavens, and laid the foundations of the earth. It was His hand that hung the worlds in space, and fashioned the flowers of the field. 'His strength setteth fast the mountains.' 'The sea is His, and He made it.' Psalm 65:6; 95:5. It was He that filled the earth with beauty, and the air with song. And upon all things in earth, and air, and sky, He wrote the message of the Father's love."

"When the woman saw that the tree was good for food, that it was pleasant
to the eyes, and a tree desirable to make one wise, she took of its fruit
and ate. She also gave to her husband with her, and he ate."
Genesis 3:6

"Eve really believed the words of Satan, but her belief did not
save her from the penalty of sin. She disbelieved the
words of God, and this was what led to her fall."
Patriarchs and Prophets, p. 55

Chapter 6
The Fall of Man

Genesis 3:1–24

"Now the serpent was more cunning than any beast of the field which the Lord God had made. And he said to the woman, 'Has God indeed said, "You shall not eat of every tree of the garden"?'

"And the woman said to the serpent, 'We may eat the fruit of the trees of the garden; but of the fruit of the tree which *is* in the midst of the garden, God has said, "You shall not eat it, nor shall you touch it, lest you die." '

"Then the serpent said to the woman, 'You will not surely die. For God knows that in the day you eat of it your eyes will be opened, and you will be like God, knowing good and evil.'

"So when the woman saw that the tree *was* good for food, that it *was* pleasant to the eyes, and a tree desirable to make *one* wise, she took of its fruit and ate. She also gave to her husband with her, and he ate. Then the eyes of both of them were opened, and they knew that they *were* naked; and they sewed fig leaves together and made themselves coverings.

"And they heard the sound of the Lord God walking in the garden in the cool of the day, and Adam and his wife hid themselves from the presence of the Lord God among the trees of the garden.

"Then the Lord God called to Adam and said to him, 'Where *are* you?'

"So he said, 'I heard Your voice in the garden, and I was afraid because I was naked; and I hid myself.'

"And He said, 'Who told you that you *were* naked? Have you eaten from the tree of which I commanded you that you should not eat?'

"Then the man said, 'The woman whom You gave *to be* with me, she gave me of the tree, and I ate.'

"And the Lord God said to the woman, 'What *is* this you have done?'

"The woman said, 'The serpent deceived me, and I ate.'

"So the Lord God said to the serpent: 'Because you have done this, you *are* cursed more than all cattle, and more than every beast of the field; on your belly you shall go, and you shall eat dust all the days of your life. And I will put enmity between you and the woman, and between your seed and her Seed; He shall bruise your head, and you shall bruise His heel.'

"To the woman He said: 'I will greatly multiply your sorrow and your conception; in pain you shall bring forth children; your desire *shall be* for your husband, and he shall rule over you.'

"Then to Adam He said, 'Because you have heeded the voice of your wife, and have eaten from the tree of which I commanded you, saying, "You shall not eat of it": Cursed *is* the ground for your sake; in toil you shall eat *of* it all the days of your life. Both thorns and thistles it shall bring forth for you, and you shall eat the herb of the field. In the sweat of your face you shall eat bread till you return to the ground, for out of it you were taken; For dust you *are*, and to dust you shall return.'

"And Adam called his wife's name Eve, because she was the mother of all living.

"Also for Adam and his wife the Lord God made tunics of skin, and clothed them.

"Then the Lord God said, 'Behold, the man has become like one of Us, to know good and evil. And now, lest he put out his hand and take also of the tree of life, and eat, and live forever'—therefore the Lord God sent him out of the garden of Eden to till the ground from which he was taken. So He drove out the man; and He placed cherubim at the east of the garden of Eden, and a flaming sword which turned every way, to guard the way to the tree of life."

Romans 5:12

"Therefore, just as through one man sin entered the world, and death through sin, and thus death spread to all men, because all sinned."

Romans 6:23

"For the wages of sin *is* death, but the gift of God *is* eternal life in Christ Jesus our Lord."

Romans 3:23

"For all have sinned and fall short of the glory of God."

Romans 7:18

"For I know that in me (that is, in my flesh) nothing good dwells; for to will is present with me, but *how* to perform what is good I do not find."

Jeremiah 17:9

"The heart *is* deceitful above all *things*, and desperately wicked; who can know it?"

James 1:14, 15

"But each one is tempted when he is drawn away by his own desires and enticed. Then, when desire has conceived, it gives birth to sin; and sin, when it is full-grown, brings forth death."

Patriarchs and Prophets, p. 52

"Our first parents were not left without a warning of the danger that threatened them. Heavenly messengers opened to them the history of Satan's fall and his plots for their destruction, unfolding more fully the nature of the divine government, which the prince of evil was trying to overthrow. It was by disobedience to the just commands of God that Satan and his host had fallen. How important, then, that Adam and Eve should honor that law by which alone it was possible for order and equity to be maintained."

> "It was by disobedience to the just commands of God that Satan and his host had fallen. How important, then, that Adam and Eve should honor that law."

Patriarchs and Prophets, p. 53

"Like the angels, the dwellers in Eden had been placed upon probation; their happy estate could be retained only on condition of fidelity to the Creator's law. They could obey and live, or disobey and perish. God had made them the recipients of rich blessings; but should they disregard His will, He who spared not the angels that sinned, could not spare them; transgression would forfeit His gifts and bring upon them misery and ruin.

"The angels warned them to be on their guard against the devices of Satan, for his efforts to ensnare them would be unwearied. While they were obedient to God the evil one could not harm them; for, if need be, every angel in heaven would be sent to their help. If they steadfastly repelled his first insinuations, they would be as secure as the heavenly messengers. But should they once yield to temptation, their nature would become so depraved that in themselves they would have no power and no disposition to resist Satan."

Patriarchs and Prophets, pp. 53–57

"In order to accomplish his work unperceived, Satan chose to employ as his medium the serpent—a disguise well adapted for his purpose of deception. The serpent was then one of the wisest and most beautiful creatures on the earth. It had wings, and while flying through the air presented an appearance of dazzling brightness, having the color and brilliancy of burnished gold. Resting in the rich-laden branches of the forbidden tree and regaling itself with the delicious fruit, it was an object to arrest the attention and delight the eye of the beholder. Thus in the garden of peace lurked the destroyer, watching for his prey.

"The angels had cautioned Eve to beware of separating herself from her husband while occupied in their daily labor in the garden; with him she would be in less danger from temptation than if she were alone. But absorbed in her pleasing task, she unconsciously wandered from his side. On perceiving that she was alone, she felt an apprehension of danger, but dismissed her fears, deciding that she had sufficient wisdom and strength to discern evil and to withstand it. Unmindful of the angels' caution, she soon found herself gazing with mingled curiosity and admiration upon the forbidden tree. The fruit was very beautiful, and she questioned with herself why God had withheld it from them. Now was the tempter's opportunity. As if he were able to discern the workings of her mind, he addressed her: 'Yea, hath God said, Ye shall not eat of every tree of the garden [Genesis 3:1]?' Eve was surprised and startled as she thus seemed to hear the echo of her thoughts. But the serpent continued, in a musical voice, with subtle praise of her surpassing loveliness; and his words were not displeasing. Instead of fleeing from the spot she lingered wonderingly to hear a serpent speak. Had she been addressed by a being like the angels, her fears would have been excited; but she had no thought that the fascinating serpent could become the medium of the fallen foe.

"To the tempter's ensnaring question she replied: 'We may eat of the fruit of the trees of the garden: but of the fruit of the tree which is in the midst of the garden, God hath said, Ye shall not eat of it, neither shall ye touch it, lest ye die. And the serpent said unto the woman, Ye shall not surely die: for God doth know that in the day ye eat thereof, then your eyes shall be opened, and ye shall be as gods, knowing good and evil [Genesis 3:2–5].'

"By partaking of this tree, he declared, they would attain to a more exalted sphere of existence and enter a broader field of knowledge. He himself had eaten of the forbidden fruit, and as a result had acquired the power of speech. And he insinuated that the Lord jealously desired to withhold it from them, lest they should be exalted to equality with Himself. It was because of its wonderful properties, imparting wisdom and power, that He had prohibited them from tasting or even touching it. The tempter intimated that the divine warning was not to be actually fulfilled; it was designed merely to intimidate them. How could it be possible for them to die? Had they not eaten of the tree of life? God had been seeking to prevent them from reaching a nobler development and finding greater happiness.

"Such has been Satan's work from the days of Adam to the present, and he has pursued it with great success. He tempts men to distrust God's love and to doubt His wisdom. He is constantly seeking to excite a spirit of irreverent curiosity, a restless, inquisitive desire to penetrate the secrets of divine wisdom and power. In their efforts to search out what God has been pleased to withhold, multitudes overlook the truths which He has revealed, and which are essential to salvation. Satan tempts men to disobedience by leading them to believe they are entering a wonderful field of knowledge. But this is all a deception. Elated with their ideas of progression, they are, by trampling on God's requirements, setting their feet in the path that leads to degradation and death.

> **"In their efforts to search out what God has been pleased to withhold, multitudes overlook the truths which He has revealed, and which are essential to salvation."**

"Satan represented to the holy pair that they would be gainers by breaking the law of God. Do we not today hear similar reasoning? Many talk of the narrowness of those who obey God's commandments, while they themselves claim to have broader ideas and to enjoy greater liberty. What is this but an echo of the voice from Eden, 'In the day ye eat thereof'—transgress the divine requirement—'ye shall be as gods [Genesis 3:5]'? Satan claimed to have received great good by eating of the forbidden fruit, but he did not let it appear that by transgression he had become an outcast from heaven. Though he had found sin to result in infinite loss, he concealed his own misery in order to draw others into the

same position. So now the transgressor seeks to disguise his true character; he may claim to be holy; but his exalted profession only makes him the more dangerous as a deceiver. He is on the side of Satan, trampling upon the law of God, and leading others to do the same, to their eternal ruin.

"Eve really believed the words of Satan, but her belief did not save her from the penalty of sin. She disbelieved the words of God, and this was what led to her fall. In the judgment men will not be condemned because they conscientiously believed a lie, but because they did not believe the truth, because they neglected the opportunity of learning what is truth. Notwithstanding the sophistry of Satan to the contrary, it is always disastrous to disobey God. We must set our hearts to know what is truth. All the lessons which God has caused to be placed on record in His word are for our warning and instruction. They are given to save us from deception. Their neglect will result in ruin to ourselves. Whatever contradicts God's word, we may be sure proceeds from Satan.

"The serpent plucked the fruit of the forbidden tree and placed it in the hands of the half-reluctant Eve. Then he reminded her of her own words, that God had forbidden them to touch it, lest they die. She would receive no more harm from eating the fruit, he declared, than from touching it. Perceiving no evil results from what she had done, Eve grew bolder. When she 'saw that the tree was good for food, and that it was pleasant to the eyes, and a tree to be desired to make one wise, she took of the fruit thereof, and did eat [Genesis 3:6].' It was grateful to the taste, and as she ate, she seemed to feel a vivifying power, and imagined herself entering upon a higher state of existence. Without a fear she plucked and ate. And now, having herself transgressed, she became the agent of Satan in working the ruin of her husband. In a state of strange, unnatural excitement, with her hands filled with the forbidden fruit, she sought his presence, and related all that had occurred.

"An expression of sadness came over the face of Adam. He appeared astonished and alarmed. To the words of Eve he replied that this must be the foe against whom they had been warned; and by the divine sentence she must die. In answer she urged him to eat, repeating the words of the serpent, that they should not surely die. She reasoned that this must be true, for she felt no evidence of God's displeasure, but on the contrary realized a delicious, exhilarating influence, thrilling every faculty with new life, such, she imagined, as inspired the heavenly messengers.

"Adam understood that his companion had transgressed the command of God, disregarded the only prohibition laid upon them as a test of their fidelity and love. There was a terrible struggle in his mind. He mourned that he had permitted Eve to wander from his side. But now the deed was done; he must be separated from her whose society had been his joy. How could he have it thus? Adam had enjoyed the companionship of God and of holy angels. He had looked upon the glory of the Creator. He understood the high destiny opened to the human race should they remain faithful to God. Yet all these blessings were lost sight of in the fear of losing that one gift which in his eyes outvalued every other. Love, gratitude, loyalty to the Creator—all were overborne by love to Eve. She was a part of himself, and he could not endure the thought of separation. He did not realize that the same Infinite Power who had from the dust of the earth created him, a living, beautiful form, and had in love given him a companion, could supply her place. He resolved to share

her fate; if she must die, he would die with her. After all, he reasoned, might not the words of the wise serpent be true? Eve was before him, as beautiful and apparently as innocent as before this act of disobedience. She expressed greater love for him than before. No sign of death appeared in her, and he decided to brave the consequences. He seized the fruit and quickly ate."

Patriarchs and Prophets, pp. 57–59

"But the great Lawgiver was about to make known to Adam and Eve the consequences of their transgression. The divine presence was manifested in the garden. In their innocence and holiness they had joyfully welcomed the approach of their Creator; but now they fled in terror, and sought to hide in the deepest recesses of the garden. But 'the Lord God called unto Adam, and said unto him, Where art thou? And he said, I heard Thy voice in the garden, and I was afraid, because I was naked; and I hid myself. And He said, Who told thee that thou wast naked? Hast thou eaten of the tree, whereof I commanded thee that thou shouldest not eat [Genesis 3:8–11]?'

"Adam could neither deny nor excuse his sin; but instead of manifesting penitence, he endeavored to cast the blame upon his wife, and thus upon God Himself: 'The woman whom *Thou gavest* to be with me, she gave me of the tree, and I did eat [Genesis 3:12].' He who, from love to Eve, had deliberately chosen to forfeit the approval of God, his home in Paradise, and an eternal life of joy, could now, after his fall, endeavor to make his companion, and even the Creator Himself, responsible for the transgression. So terrible is the power of sin.

"When the woman was asked, 'What is this that thou hast done?' she answered, 'The serpent beguiled me, and I did eat [Genesis

3:13].' 'Why didst Thou create the serpent? Why didst Thou suffer him to enter Eden?'—these were the questions implied in her excuse for her sin. Thus, like Adam, she charged God with the responsibility of their fall. The spirit of self-justification originated in the father of lies; it was indulged by our first parents as soon as they yielded to the influence of Satan, and has been exhibited by all the sons and daughters of Adam. Instead of humbly confessing their sins, they try to shield themselves by casting the blame upon others, upon circumstances, or upon God—making even His blessings an occasion of murmuring against Him.

"The Lord then passed sentence upon the serpent: 'Because thou hast done this, thou art cursed above all cattle, and above every beast of the field; upon thy belly shalt thou go, and dust shalt thou eat all the days of thy life [Genesis 3:14].' Since it had been employed as Satan's medium, the serpent was to share the visitation of divine judgment. From the most beautiful and admired of the creatures of the field, it was to become the most groveling and detested of them all, feared and hated by both man and beast. The words next addressed to the serpent applied directly to Satan himself, pointing forward to his ultimate defeat and destruction: 'I will put enmity between thee and the woman, and between thy seed and her seed; it shall bruise thy head, and thou shalt bruise his heel [Genesis 3:15].'

"Eve was told of the sorrow and pain that must henceforth be her portion. And the Lord said, 'Thy desire shall be to thy husband, and he shall rule over thee [Genesis 3:16].' In the creation God had made her the equal of Adam. Had they remained obedient to God—in harmony with His great law of love—they would ever have been in harmony with each other; but sin had brought discord, and now their union could be maintained and harmony preserved only by submission on the part of the one or the other. Eve had been the first in transgression; and she had fallen into temptation by separating from her companion, contrary to the divine direction. It was by her solicitation that Adam sinned, and she was now placed in subjection to her husband. Had the principles joined in the law of God been cherished by the fallen race, this sentence, though growing out of the results of sin, would have proved a blessing to them; but man's abuse of the supremacy thus given him has too often rendered the lot of woman very bitter and made her life a burden."

***Patriarchs and Prophets*, pp. 59, 60**
"To Adam the Lord declared: 'Because thou hast hearkened unto the voice of thy wife, and hast eaten of the tree, of which I commanded thee, saying, Thou shalt not eat of it: cursed is the ground for thy sake; in sorrow shalt thou eat of it all the days of thy life; thorns also and thistles shall it bring forth to thee; and thou shalt eat the herb of the field; in the sweat of thy face shalt thou eat bread, till thou return unto the ground; for out of it wast thou taken: for dust thou art, and unto dust shalt thou return [Genesis 3:17–19].'

"It was not the will of God that the sinless pair should know aught of evil. He had freely given them the good, and had withheld the evil. But, contrary to His command, they had eaten of the forbidden tree, and now they would continue to eat of it—they would have the knowledge of evil—all the days of their life. From that time the race would be afflicted by Satan's temptations. Instead of the happy labor heretofore appointed them, anxiety and toil were to be their lot. They would be subject to disappointment, grief, and pain, and finally to death.

"Under the curse of sin all nature was to witness to man of the character and results of rebellion against God. When God made man He made him rule over the earth and all living creatures. So long as Adam remained loyal to Heaven, all nature was in subjection to him. But when he rebelled against the divine law, the inferior creatures were in rebellion against his rule. Thus the Lord, in His great mercy, would show men the sacredness of His law, and lead them, by their own experience, to see the danger of setting it aside, even in the slightest degree."

Genesis 2:17
"But of the tree of the knowledge of good and evil you shall not eat, for in the day that you eat of it you shall surely die."

Patriarchs and Prophets, p. 60
"The warning given to our first parents—'In the day that thou eatest thereof thou shalt surely die' (Genesis 2:17)—did not imply that they were to die on the very day when they partook of the forbidden fruit. But on that day the irrevocable sentence would be pronounced. Immortality was promised them on condition of obedience; by transgression they would forfeit eternal life. That very day they would be doomed to death."

Patriarchs and Prophets, p. 61
"To Eve it seemed a small thing to disobey God by tasting the fruit of the forbidden tree, and to tempt her husband also to transgress; but their sin opened the floodgates of woe upon the world. Who can know, in the moment of temptation, the terrible consequences that will result from one wrong step? …

"After their sin Adam and Eve were no longer to dwell in Eden. They earnestly entreated that they might remain in the home of their innocence and joy. They confessed that they had forfeited all right to that happy abode, but pledged themselves for the future to yield strict obedience to God. But they were told that their nature had become depraved by sin; they had lessened their strength to resist evil and had opened the way for Satan to gain more ready access to them. In their innocence they had yielded to temptation; and now, in a state of conscious guilt, they would have less power to maintain their integrity.

"In humility and unutterable sadness they bade farewell to their beautiful home and went forth to dwell upon the earth, where rested the curse of sin. The atmosphere, once so mild and uniform in temperature, was now subject to marked changes, and the Lord mercifully provided them with a garment of skins as a protection from the extremes of heat and cold."

Colossians 2:3
"In whom are hidden all the treasures of wisdom and knowledge."

Steps to Christ, pp. 17, 18
"Man was originally endowed with noble powers and a well-balanced mind. He was perfect in his being, and in harmony with God. His thoughts were pure, his aims holy. But through disobedience, his powers were perverted, and selfishness took the place of love. His nature became so weakened through transgression that it was impossible for him, in his own strength, to resist the power of evil. He was made captive by Satan, and would have remained so forever had not God specially interposed. It was the tempter's purpose to thwart the divine plan in man's creation, and fill the earth with woe and desolation. And he would point to all this evil as the result of God's work in creating man.

"In his sinless state, man held joyful communion with Him 'in whom are hid all the treasures of wisdom and knowledge.' Colossians 2:3. But after his sin, he could no longer find joy in holiness, and he sought to hide from the presence of God. Such is still the condition of the unrenewed heart. It is not in harmony with God, and finds no joy in communion with Him. The sinner could not be happy in God's presence; he would shrink from the companionship of holy beings. Could he be permitted to enter heaven, it would have no joy for him. The spirit of unselfish love that reigns there— every heart responding to the heart of Infinite Love—would touch no answering chord in his soul. His thoughts, his interests, his motives, would be alien to those that actuate the sinless dwellers there. He would be a discordant note in the melody of heaven. Heaven would be to him a place of torture; he would long to be hidden from Him who is its light, and the center of its joy. It is no arbitrary decree on the part of God that excludes the wicked from heaven; they are shut out by their own unfitness for its companionship. The glory of God would be to them a consuming fire. They would welcome destruction, that they might be hidden from the face of Him who died to redeem them."

"For the living know that they will die; but the dead know nothing, and they have no more reward, for the memory of them is forgotten."
Ecclesiastes 9:5

"Upon the fundamental error of natural immortality rests the doctrine of consciousness in death—a doctrine, like eternal torment, opposed to the teachings of the Scriptures, to the dictates of reason, and to our feelings of humanity."
The Great Controversy, p. 545

Chapter 7

The Non-Immortality of the Wicked

Ezekiel 18:4

"Behold, all souls are Mine; the soul of the father as well as the soul of the son is Mine; the soul who sins shall die."

1 Samuel 28:6

"And when Saul inquired of the Lord, the Lord did not answer him, either by dreams or by Urim or by the prophets."

1 Chronicles 10:13, 14

"Saul died for his unfaithfulness which he had committed against the Lord, because he did not keep the word of the Lord, and also because he consulted a medium for guidance. But *he* did not inquire of the Lord; therefore He killed him, and turned the kingdom over to David the son of Jesse."

Isaiah 8:19

"And when they say to you, 'Seek those who are mediums and wizards, who whisper and mutter,' should not a people seek their God? *Should they seek* the dead on behalf of the living?"

Numbers 25:1–3

"Now Israel remained in Acacia Grove, and the people began to commit harlotry with the women of Moab. They invited the people to the sacrifices of their gods, and the people ate and bowed down to their gods. So Israel was joined to Baal of Peor, and the anger of the Lord was aroused against Israel."

Psalm 106:28

"They joined themselves also to Baal of Peor, and ate sacrifices made to the dead."

***Patriarchs and Prophets*, pp. 683–685**

"The Scripture account of Saul's visit to the woman of Endor has been a source of perplexity to many students of the Bible. There are some who take the position that Samuel was actually present at the interview with Saul, but the Bible itself furnishes sufficient ground for a contrary conclusion. If, as claimed by some, Samuel was in heaven, he must have been summoned thence, either by the power of God or by that of Satan. None can believe for a moment that Satan had power to call the holy prophet of God from heaven to honor the incantations of an abandoned woman. Nor can we conclude that God summoned him to the witch's cave; for the Lord had already refused to communicate with Saul, by dreams, by Urim, or by prophets. 1 Samuel 28:6. These were God's own appointed mediums of communication, and He did not pass them by to deliver the message through the agent of Satan.

"The message itself is sufficient evidence of its origin. Its object was not to lead Saul to repentance, but to urge him on to ruin; and this is not the work of God, but of Satan. Furthermore, the act of Saul in consulting a sorceress is cited in Scripture as one reason why he was rejected by God and abandoned to destruction: 'Saul died for his transgression which he committed against the Lord, even against the word of the Lord, which he kept not, and also for asking counsel of one that had a familiar spirit, *to inquire of it*; and inquired not of the Lord: therefore He slew him, and turned the kingdom unto David the son of Jesse.' 1 Chronicles 10:13, 14. Here it is distinctly stated that Saul inquired of the familiar spirit, not of the Lord. He did not communicate with Samuel, the prophet of God; but through the sorceress he held intercourse with Satan. Satan could not present the real Samuel, but he did present a counterfeit, that served his purpose of deception.

"Nearly all forms of ancient sorcery and witchcraft were founded upon a belief in communion with the dead. Those who practiced the arts of necromancy claimed to have intercourse with departed spirits, and to obtain through them a knowledge of future events. This custom of consulting the dead is referred to in the prophecy of Isaiah: 'When they shall say unto you, Seek unto them that have familiar spirits, and unto wizards that peep and that mutter: should not a people seek unto their God? *for the living to the dead*?' Isaiah 8:19.

"This same belief in communion with the dead formed the cornerstone of heathen idolatry. The gods of the heathen were believed to be the deified spirits of departed heroes. Thus the religion of the heathen was a worship of the dead. This is evident from the Scriptures. In the account of the sin of Israel at Bethpeor, it is stated: 'Israel abode in Shittim, and the people began to commit whoredom with the daughters of Moab. And they called the people unto the sacrifices of their gods: and the people did eat, and bowed down to their gods. And Israel joined himself unto Baalpeor.' Numbers 25:1–3. The psalmist tells us to what kind of gods these sacrifices were offered. Speaking of the same apostasy of the Israelites, he says, 'They joined themselves also unto Baalpeor, and *ate the sacrifices of the dead*' (Psalm 106:28); that is, sacrifices that had been offered to the dead.

"The deification of the dead has held a prominent place in nearly every system of heathenism, as has also the supposed communion with the dead. The gods were believed to communicate their will to men, and also, when consulted, to give them counsel. Of this character were the famous oracles of Greece and Rome.

"The belief in communion with the dead is still held, even in professedly Christian lands. Under the name of spiritualism the practice of communicating with beings claiming to be the spirits of the departed has become widespread. It is calculated to take hold of the sympathies of those who have laid their loved ones in the grave. Spiritual beings sometimes appear to persons in the form of their deceased friends, and relate incidents connected with their lives and perform acts which they performed while living. In this way they lead men to believe that their dead friends are angels, hovering over them and communicating with them. Those who thus assume to be the spirits of the departed are regarded with a certain idolatry, and with many their word has greater weight than the word of God."

Revelation 12:10–12

"Then I heard a loud voice saying in heaven, 'Now salvation, and strength, and the kingdom of our God, and the power of His Christ have come, for the accuser of our brethren, who accused them before our God day and night, has been cast down. ... Therefore rejoice, O heavens, and you who dwell in them! Woe to the inhabitants of the earth and the sea! For the devil has come down to you, having great wrath, because he knows that he has a short time.' "

Mark 14:38
"Watch and pray, lest you enter into temptation. The spirit indeed *is* willing, but the flesh *is* weak."

Leviticus 19:31
"Give no regard to mediums and familiar spirits; do not seek after them, to be defiled by them: I *am* the Lord your God."

Deuteronomy 18:12
"For all who do these things *are* an abomination to the Lord, and because of these abominations the Lord your God drives them out from before you."

Patriarchs and Prophets, **pp. 688, 689**
"Satan was determined to keep his hold on the land of Canaan, and when it was made the habitation of the children of Israel, and the law of God was made the law of the land, he hated Israel with a cruel and malignant hatred and plotted their destruction. Through the agency of evil spirits strange gods were introduced; and because of transgression, the chosen people were finally scattered from the Land of Promise. This history Satan is striving to repeat in our day. God is leading His people out from the abominations of the world, that they may keep His law; and because of this, the rage of 'the accuser of our brethren' knows no bounds. 'The devil is come down unto you, having great wrath, because he knoweth that he hath but a short time.' Revelation 12:10, 12. The antitypical land of promise is just before us, and Satan is determined to destroy the people of God and cut them off from their inheritance. The admonition, 'Watch ye and pray, lest ye enter into temptation' (Mark 14:38), was never more needed than now."

"The word of the Lord to ancient Israel is addressed also to His people in this age: 'Regard not them that have familiar spirits, neither seek after wizards, to be defiled by them;' 'for all that do these things are an abomination unto the Lord.' Leviticus 19:31; Deuteronomy 18:12."

Genesis 2:17
"But of the tree of the knowledge of good and evil you shall not eat, for in the day that you eat of it you shall surely die."

Genesis 3:19
"In the sweat of your face you shall eat bread till you return to the ground, for out of it you were taken; for dust you *are*, and to dust you shall return."

Genesis 3:5
"For God knows that in the day you eat of it your eyes will be opened, and you will be like God, knowing good and evil."

Romans 5:12
"Therefore, just as through one man sin entered the world, and death through sin, and thus death spread to all men, because all sinned."

2 Timothy 1:10
"But has now been revealed by the appearing of our Savior Jesus Christ, *who* has abolished death and brought life and immortality to light through the gospel."

John 3:36
"He who believes in the Son has everlasting life; and he who does not believe the Son shall not see life, but the wrath of God abides on him."

Romans 2:7

"Eternal life to those who by patient continuance in doing good seek for glory, honor, and immortality."

The Great Controversy, pp. 532, 533

"But what did Adam, after his sin, find to be the meaning of the words, 'In the day that thou eatest thereof thou shalt surely die [Genesis 2:17]'? Did he find them to mean, as Satan had led him to believe, that he was to be ushered into a more exalted state of existence? Then indeed there was great good to be gained by transgression, and Satan was proved to be a benefactor of the race. But Adam did not find this to be the meaning of the divine sentence. God declared that as a penalty for his sin, man should return to the ground whence he was taken: 'Dust thou art, and unto dust shalt thou return.' [Genesis 3] Verse 19. The words of Satan, 'Your eyes shall be opened [Genesis 3:5],' proved to be true in this sense only: After Adam and Eve had disobeyed God, their eyes were opened to discern their folly; they did know evil, and they tasted the bitter fruit of transgression.

"In the midst of Eden grew the tree of life, whose fruit had the power of perpetuating life. Had Adam remained obedient to God, he would have continued to enjoy free access to this tree and would have lived forever. But when he sinned he was cut off from partaking of the tree of life, and he became subject to death. The divine sentence, 'Dust thou art, and unto dust shalt thou return,' points to the utter extinction of life.

"Immortality, promised to man on condition of obedience, had been forfeited by transgression. Adam could not transmit to his posterity that which he did not possess; and there could have been no hope for the fallen race had not God, by the sacrifice of His Son,

brought immortality within their reach. While 'death passed upon all men, for that all have sinned,' Christ 'hath brought life and immortality to light through the gospel.' Romans 5:12; 2 Timothy 1:10. And only through Christ can immortality be obtained. Said Jesus: 'He that believeth on the Son hath everlasting life: and he that believeth not the Son shall not see life.' John 3:36. Every man may come into possession of this priceless blessing if he will comply with the conditions. All 'who by patient continuance in well-doing seek for glory and honor and immortality,' will receive 'eternal life.' Romans 2:7."

> **"God declared that as a penalty for his sin, man should return to the ground whence he was taken: 'Dust thou art, and unto dust shalt thou return.'"**

The Great Controversy, p. 534

"But after the Fall, Satan bade his angels make a special effort to inculcate the belief in man's natural immortality; and having induced the people to receive this error, they were to lead them on to conclude that the sinner would live in eternal misery. Now the prince of darkness, working through his agents, represents God as a revengeful tyrant, declaring that He plunges into hell all those who do not please Him, and causes them ever to feel His wrath; and that while they suffer unutterable anguish and writhe in the eternal flames, their Creator looks down upon them with satisfaction.

"Thus the archfiend clothes with his own attributes the Creator and Benefactor of mankind. Cruelty is satanic. God is love; and all that He created was pure, holy, and lovely, until sin was brought in by the first great rebel. Satan himself is the enemy who tempts man to sin, and then destroys him if he can; and when he has made sure of his victim, then he exults in the ruin he has wrought. If permitted, he would sweep the entire race into his net. Were it not for the interposition of divine power, not one son or daughter of Adam would escape.

"Satan is seeking to overcome men today, as he overcame our first parents, by shaking their confidence in their Creator and leading them to doubt the wisdom of His government and the justice of His laws. Satan and his emissaries represent God as even worse than themselves, in order to justify their own malignity and rebellion. The great deceiver endeavors to shift his own horrible cruelty of character upon our heavenly Father, that he may cause himself to appear as one greatly wronged by his expulsion from heaven because he would not submit to so unjust a governor."

Revelation 14:8
"And another angel followed, saying, 'Babylon is fallen, is fallen, that great city, because she has made all nations drink of the wine of the wrath of her fornication.' "

Revelation 17:2
"With whom the kings of the earth committed fornication, and the inhabitants of the earth were made drunk with the wine of her fornication."

The Great Controversy, pp. 536, 537
"The theory of eternal torment is one of the false doctrines that constitute the wine of the abomination of Babylon, of which she makes all nations drink. Revelation 14:8; 17:2. That ministers of Christ should have accepted this heresy and proclaimed it from the sacred desk is indeed a mystery. They received it from

Rome, as they received the false sabbath. True, it has been taught by great and good men; but the light on this subject had not come to them as it has come to us. They were responsible only for the light which shone in their time; we are accountable for that which shines in our day. If we turn from the testimony of God's word, and accept false doctrines because our fathers taught them, we fall under the condemnation pronounced upon Babylon; we are drinking of the wine of her abomination."

Acts 24:15
"I have hope in God, which they themselves also accept, that there will be a resurrection of *the* dead, both of *the* just and *the* unjust."

1 Corinthians 15:22
"For as in Adam all die, even so in Christ all shall be made alive."

John 5:28, 29
"Do not marvel at this; for the hour is coming in which all who are in the graves will hear His voice and come forth—those who have done good, to the resurrection of life, and those who have done evil, to the resurrection of condemnation."

Revelation 20:6
"Blessed and holy *is* he who has part in the first resurrection. Over such the second death has no power, but they shall be priests of God and of Christ, and shall reign with Him a thousand years."

Romans 6:23
"For the wages of sin *is* death, but the gift of God *is* eternal life in Christ Jesus our Lord."

Revelation 20:13

"The sea gave up the dead who were in it, and Death and Hades delivered up the dead who were in them. And they were judged, each one according to his works."

Psalm 37:10

"For yet a little while and the wicked *shall be* no *more*; indeed, you will look carefully for his place, but it *shall be* no *more*."

Obadiah 16

"For as you drank on My holy mountain, *So* shall all the nations drink continually; yes, they shall drink, and swallow, and they shall be as though they had never been."

Psalm 9:5, 6

"You have rebuked the nations, You have destroyed the wicked; You have blotted out their name forever and ever. O enemy, destructions are finished forever! And you have destroyed cities; even their memory has perished."

Revelation 5:13

"And every creature which is in heaven and on the earth and under the earth and such as are in the sea, and all that are in them, I heard saying: 'Blessing and honor and glory and power *be* to Him who sits on the throne, and to the Lamb, forever and ever!' "

Psalm 146:4

"His spirit departs, he returns to his earth; in that very day his plans perish."

Ecclesiastes 9:5, 6, 10

"For the living know that they will die; but the dead know nothing, and they have no more reward, for the memory of them is forgotten. Also their love, their hatred, and their envy have now perished; nevermore will they have a share in anything done under the sun."

"Whatever your hand finds to do, do *it* with your might; for *there is* no work or device or knowledge or wisdom in the grave where you are going."

Isaiah 38:18, 19

"For Sheol cannot thank You, death cannot praise You; those who go down to the pit cannot hope for Your truth. The living, the living man, he shall praise You, as I *do* this day; the father shall make known Your truth to the children."

Psalm 6:5

"For in death *there is* no remembrance of You; in the grave who will give You thanks?"

Psalm 115:17

"The dead do not praise the Lord, nor any who go down into silence."

Acts 2:29, 34

"Men *and* brethren, let *me* speak freely to you of the patriarch David, that he is both dead and buried, and his tomb is with us to this day."

"For David did not ascend into the heavens, but he says himself: 'The Lord said to my Lord, "Sit at My right hand." ' "

1 Corinthians 15:16–18

"For if *the* dead do not rise, then Christ is not risen. And if Christ is not risen, your faith *is* futile; you are still in your sins! Then also those who have fallen asleep in Christ have perished."

The Great Controversy, pp. 544–547

"In consequence of Adam's sin, death passed upon the whole human race. All alike go down into the grave. And through the provisions of the plan of salvation, all are to be brought forth from their graves. 'There shall be a resurrection of the dead, both of the just and unjust;' 'for as in Adam all die, even so in Christ shall all be made alive.' Acts 24:15; 1 Corinthians 15:22. But a distinction is made between the two classes that are brought forth. 'All that are in the graves shall hear His voice, and shall come forth; they that have done good, unto the resurrection of life; and they that have done evil, unto the resurrection of damnation.' John 5:28, 29. They who have been 'accounted worthy' of the resurrection of life are 'blessed and holy.' 'On such the second death hath no power.' Revelation 20:6. But those who have not, through repentance and faith, secured pardon, must receive the penalty of transgression—'the wages of sin [Romans 6:23].' They suffer punishment varying in duration and intensity, 'according to their works [Revelation 20:13],' but finally ending in the second death. Since it is impossible for God, consistently with His justice and mercy, to save the sinner in his sins, He deprives him of the existence which his transgressions have forfeited and of which he has proved himself unworthy. Says an inspired writer: 'Yet a little while, and the wicked shall not be: yea, thou shalt diligently consider his place, and it shall not be.' And another declares: 'They shall be as though they had not been.' Psalm 37:10; Obadiah 16. Covered with infamy, they sink into hopeless, eternal oblivion.

"Thus will be made an end of sin, with all the woe and ruin which have resulted from it. Says the psalmist: 'Thou hast destroyed the wicked, Thou hast put out their name forever and ever. O thou enemy, destructions are come to a perpetual end.' Psalm 9:5, 6. John, in the Revelation, looking forward to the eternal state, hears a universal anthem of praise undisturbed by one note of discord.

Every creature in heaven and earth was heard ascribing glory to God. Revelation 5:13. There will then be no lost souls to blaspheme God as they writhe in never-ending torment; no wretched beings in hell will mingle their shrieks with the songs of the saved.

> **"All that are in the graves shall hear His voice, and shall come forth; ... they that have done evil, unto the resurrection of damnation."**

"Upon the fundamental error of natural immortality rests the doctrine of consciousness in death—a doctrine, like eternal torment, opposed to the teachings of the Scriptures, to the dictates of reason, and to our feelings of humanity. According to the popular belief, the redeemed in heaven are acquainted with all that takes place on the earth and especially with the lives of the friends whom they have left behind. But how could it be a source of happiness to the dead to know the troubles of the living, to witness the sins committed by their own loved ones, and to see them enduring all the sorrows, disappointments, and anguish of life? How much of heaven's bliss would be enjoyed by those who were hovering over their friends on earth? And how utterly revolting is the belief that as soon as the breath leaves the body the soul of the impenitent is consigned to the flames of hell! To what depths of anguish must those be plunged who see their friends passing to the grave unprepared, to enter upon an eternity of woe and sin! Many have been driven to insanity by this harrowing thought.

"What say the Scriptures concerning these things? David declares that man is not conscious in death. 'His breath goeth forth, he returneth to his earth; in that very day his thoughts perish.' Psalm 146:4. Solomon bears the same testimony: 'The living know that they shall die: but the dead know not anything.' 'Their love, and their hatred, and their envy, is now perished; neither have they any more a portion forever in anything that is done under the sun.' 'There is no work, nor device, nor knowledge, nor wisdom, in the grave, whither thou goest.' Ecclesiastes 9:5, 6, 10.

"When, in answer to his prayer, Hezekiah's life was prolonged fifteen years, the grateful king rendered to God a tribute of praise for His great mercy. In this song he tells the reason why he thus rejoices: 'The grave cannot praise Thee, death cannot celebrate Thee: they that go down into the pit cannot hope for Thy truth. The living, the living, he shall praise Thee, as I do this day.' Isaiah 38:18, 19. Popular theology represents the righteous dead as in heaven, entered into bliss and praising God with an immortal tongue; but Hezekiah could see no such glorious prospect in death. With his words agrees the testimony of the psalmist: 'In death there is no remembrance of Thee: in the grave who shall give Thee thanks?' 'The dead praise not the Lord, neither any that go down into silence.' Psalm 6:5; 115:17.

"Peter on the Day of Pentecost declared that the patriarch David 'is both dead and buried, and his sepulcher is with us unto this day.' 'For David is not ascended into the heavens.' Acts 2:29, 34. The fact that David remains in the grave until the resurrection proves that the righteous do not go to heaven at death. It is only through the resurrection, and by virtue of the fact that Christ has risen, that David can at last sit at the right hand of God.

"And said Paul: 'If the dead rise not, then is not Christ raised: and if Christ be not raised, your faith is vain; ye are yet in your sins. Then

they also which are fallen asleep in Christ are perished.' 1 Corinthians 15:16–18. If for four thousand years the righteous had gone directly to heaven at death, how could Paul have said that if there is no resurrection, 'they also which are fallen asleep in Christ are perished'? No resurrection would be necessary."

1 Thessalonians 4:14

"For if we believe that Jesus died and rose again, even so God will bring with Him those who sleep in Jesus."

Job 14:10–12

"But man dies and is laid away; indeed he breathes his last and where *is* he? *As* water disappears from the sea, and a river becomes parched and dries up, so man lies down and does not rise. Till the heavens *are* no more, they will not awake nor be roused from their sleep."

Ecclesiastes 12:6

"*Remember your Creator* before the silver cord is loosed, or the golden bowl is broken, or the pitcher shattered at the fountain, or the wheel broken at the well."

Job 14:21

"His sons come to honor, and he does not know *it*; they are brought low, and he does not perceive *it*."

1 Corinthians 15:52–55

"In a moment, in the twinkling of an eye, at the last trumpet. For the trumpet will sound, and the dead will be raised incorruptible, and we shall be changed. For this corruptible must put on incorruption, and this mortal *must* put on immortality. So when this corruptible has put on incorruption, and this mortal has put on immortality, then shall be brought to pass the saying that is written: 'Death is swallowed up in victory.'

" 'O Death, where *is* your sting? O Hades, where *is* your victory?' "

The Great Controversy, pp. 549, 550

"The theory of the immortality of the soul was one of those false doctrines that Rome, borrowing from paganism, incorporated into the religion of Christendom. Martin Luther classed it with the 'monstrous fables that form part of the Roman dunghill of decretals.'—E. Petavel, *The Problem of Immortality*, page 255. Commenting on the words of Solomon in Ecclesiastes, that the dead know not anything, the Reformer says: 'Another place proving that the dead have no … feeling. There is, saith he, no duty, no science, no knowledge, no wisdom there. Solomon judgeth that the dead are asleep, and feel nothing at all. For the dead lie there, accounting neither days nor years, but when they are awaked, they shall seem to have slept scarce one minute.'—Martin Luther, *Exposition of Solomon's Booke Called Ecclesiastes*, page 152.

"Nowhere in the Sacred Scriptures is found the statement that the righteous go to their reward or the wicked to their punishment at death. The patriarchs and prophets have left no such assurance. Christ and His apostles have given no hint of it. The Bible clearly teaches that the dead do not go immediately to heaven. They are represented as sleeping until the resurrection. 1 Thessalonians 4:14; Job 14:10–12. In the very day when the silver cord is loosed and the golden bowl broken (Ecclesiastes 12:6), man's thoughts perish. They that go down to the grave are in silence. They know no more of anything that is done under the sun. Job 14:21. Blessed rest for the weary righteous! Time, be it long or short, is but a moment to them. They sleep; they are awakened by the trump of God to a glorious immortality. 'For the trumpet shall sound, and the dead shall be raised incorruptible.… So when this corruptible shall have put on incorruption, and this mortal shall have put on immortality, then shall be brought to pass the saying that is written, Death is swallowed up in victory.' 1 Corinthians 15:52–54. As they are called forth from their deep slumber they begin to think just where they ceased. The last sensation was the pang of death; the last thought, that they were falling beneath the power of the grave. When they arise from the tomb, their first glad thought will be echoed in the triumphal shout: 'O death, where is thy sting? O grave, where is thy victory?' Verse 55."

Hebrews 1:14

"Are they not all ministering spirits sent forth to minister for those who will inherit salvation?"

1 Timothy 4:1

"Now the Spirit expressly says that in latter times some will depart from the faith, giving heed to deceiving spirits and doctrines of demons."

The Great Controversy, pp. 551–553

"The doctrine of natural immortality, first borrowed from the pagan philosophy, and in the darkness of the great apostasy incorporated into the Christian faith, has supplanted the truth, so plainly taught in Scripture, that 'the dead know not anything [Ecclesiastes 9:5].' Multitudes have come to believe that it is spirits of the dead who are the 'ministering spirits, sent forth to minister for them who shall be heirs of salvation [Hebrews 1:14].' And this notwithstanding the testimony of Scripture to the existence of heavenly angels, and their connection with the history of man, before the death of a human being.

"The doctrine of man's consciousness in death, especially the belief that spirits of the dead return to minister to the living, has prepared the way for modern spiritualism. If the dead are admitted to the presence of God and holy angels, and privileged with knowledge far exceeding what they before possessed, why should they not return to the earth to enlighten and instruct the living? If, as taught by popular theologians, spirits of the dead are hovering about their friends on earth, why should they not be permitted to communicate with them, to warn them against evil, or to comfort them in sorrow? How can those who believe in man's consciousness in death reject what comes to them as divine light communicated by glorified spirits? Here is a channel regarded as sacred, through which Satan works for the accomplishment of his purposes. The fallen angels who do his bidding appear as messengers from the spirit world. While professing to bring the living into communication with the dead, the prince of evil exercises his bewitching influence upon their minds.

"He has power to bring before men the appearance of their departed friends. The counterfeit is perfect; the familiar look, the words, the tone, are reproduced with marvelous distinctness. Many are comforted with the assurance that their loved ones are enjoying the bliss of heaven, and without suspicion of danger, they give ear 'to seducing spirits, and doctrines of devils [1 Timothy 4:1].'

"When they have been led to believe that the dead actually return to communicate with them, Satan causes those to appear who went into the grave unprepared. They claim to be happy in heaven and even to occupy exalted positions there, and thus the error is widely taught that no difference is made between the righteous and the wicked. The pretended visitants from the world of spirits sometimes

utter cautions and warnings which prove to be correct. Then, as confidence is gained, they present doctrines that directly undermine faith in the Scriptures. With an appearance of deep interest in the well-being of their friends on earth, they insinuate the most dangerous errors. The fact that they state some truths, and are able at times to foretell future events, gives to their statements an appearance of reliability; and their false teachings are accepted by the multitudes as readily, and believed as implicitly, as if they were the most sacred truths of the Bible. The law of God is set aside, the Spirit of grace despised, the blood of the covenant counted an unholy thing. The spirits deny the deity of Christ and place even the Creator on a level with themselves. Thus under a new disguise the great rebel still carries on his warfare against God, begun in heaven and for nearly six thousand years continued upon the earth."

Revelation 3:10
"Because you have kept My command to persevere, I also will keep you from the hour of trial which shall come upon the whole world, to test those who dwell on the earth."

The Great Controversy, p. 560
"Many will be confronted by the spirits of devils personating beloved relatives or friends and declaring the most dangerous heresies. These visitants will appeal to our tenderest sympathies and will work miracles to sustain their pretensions. We must be prepared to withstand them with the Bible truth that the dead know not anything and that they who thus appear are the spirits of devils.

"Just before us is 'the hour of temptation, which shall come upon all the world, to try them that dwell upon the earth.' Revelation 3:10. All whose faith is not firmly established upon the word of God will be deceived and overcome. Satan 'works with all deceivableness of unrighteousness' to gain control of the children of men, and his deceptions will continually increase. But he can gain his object only as men voluntarily yield to his temptations. Those who are earnestly seeking a knowledge of the truth and are striving to purify their souls through obedience, thus doing what they can to prepare for the conflict, will find, in the God of truth, a sure defense."

"If we confess our sins, He is faithful and just to forgive us
our sins and to cleanse us from all unrighteousness."
1 John 1:9

"We are now living in the great day of atonement.... All who would
have their names retained in the book of life should now, in the
few remaining days of their probation, afflict their souls
before God by sorrow for sin and true repentance."
The Great Controversy, p. 490

Chapter 8

The Atonement

Romans 3:23

"For all have sinned and fall short of the glory of God."

Romans 6:23

"For the wages of sin *is* death, but the gift of God *is* eternal life in Christ Jesus our Lord."

1 John 1:9

"If we confess our sins, He is faithful and just to forgive us *our* sins and to cleanse us from all unrighteousness."

At the Cross

***Patriarchs and Prophets*, p. 63**

"The broken law of God demanded the life of the sinner. In all the universe there was but one who could, in behalf of man, satisfy its claims. Since the divine law is as sacred as God Himself, only one equal with God could make atonement for its transgression. None but Christ could redeem fallen man from the curse of the law and bring him again into harmony with Heaven. Christ would take upon Himself the guilt and shame of sin—sin so offensive to a holy God that it must separate the Father and His Son. Christ would reach to the depths of misery to rescue the ruined race."

Revelation 13:8

"All who dwell on the earth will worship him [the beast], whose names have not been written in the Book of Life of the Lamb slain from the foundation of the world."

John 3:14–17

"And as Moses lifted up the serpent in the wilderness, even so must the Son of Man be lifted up, that whoever believes in Him should not perish but have eternal life. For God so loved the world that He gave His only begotten Son, that whoever believes in Him should not perish but have everlasting life. For God did not send His Son into the world to condemn the world, but that the world through Him might be saved.."

"The plan of salvation had been laid before the creation of the earth; for Christ is 'the Lamb slain from the foundation of the world' (Revelation 13:8)."

***Patriarchs and Prophets*, p. 63**

"The plan of salvation had been laid before the creation of the earth; for Christ is 'the Lamb slain from the foundation of the world' (Revelation 13:8); yet it was a struggle, even with the King of the universe, to yield up His Son to die for the guilty race. But 'God so loved the world, that He gave His only-begotten Son, that whosoever believeth in Him should not perish, but have everlasting life.' John 3:16."

Daniel 9:26, 27

"And after the sixty-two weeks Messiah shall be cut off, but not for Himself; ... He shall confirm a covenant with many for one week; but in the middle of the week He shall bring an end to sacrifice and offering."

2 Corinthians 5:18–21
"Now all things *are* of God, who has reconciled us to Himself through Jesus Christ, and has given us the ministry of reconciliation, that is, that God was in Christ reconciling the world to Himself, not imputing their trespasses to them, and has committed to us the word of reconciliation.… For He made Him who knew no sin *to be* sin for us, that we might become the righteousness of God in Him."

1 John 3:2
"Beloved, now we are children of God; and it has not yet been revealed what we shall be, but we know that when He is revealed, we shall be like Him, for we shall see Him as He is."

Patriarchs and Prophets, **p. 64**
"God was to be manifest in Christ, 'reconciling the world unto Himself.' 2 Corinthians 5:19. Man had become so degraded by sin that it was impossible for him, in himself, to come into harmony with Him whose nature is purity and goodness. But Christ, after having redeemed man from the condemnation of the law, could impart divine power to unite with human effort. Thus by repentance toward God and faith in Christ the fallen children of Adam might once more become 'sons of God.' 1 John 3:2."

Genesis 3:15
"And I will put enmity between you and the woman, and between your seed and her Seed; He shall bruise your head, and you shall bruise His heel."

The Great Controversy, **pp. 347, 348**
"The kingdom of grace was instituted immediately after the fall of man, when a plan was devised for the redemption of the guilty race. It then existed in the purpose and by the promise of God; and through faith, men could become its subjects. Yet it was not actually established until the death of Christ. Even after entering upon His earthly mission, the Saviour, wearied with the stubbornness and ingratitude of men, might have drawn back from the sacrifice of Calvary. In Gethsemane the cup of woe trembled in His hand. He might even then have wiped the blood-sweat from His brow and have left the guilty race to perish in their iniquity. Had He done this, there could have been no redemption for fallen men. But when the Saviour yielded up His life, and with His expiring breath cried out, 'It is finished,' then the fulfillment of the plan of redemption was assured. The promise of salvation made to the sinful pair in Eden was ratified. The kingdom of grace, which had before existed by the promise of God, was then established."

John 19:30
"So when Jesus had received the sour wine, He said, 'It is finished!' And bowing His head, He gave up His spirit."

Matthew 27:50, 51 (see also Mark 15:37; Luke 23:45, 46)
"And Jesus cried out again with a loud voice, and yielded up His spirit. Then, behold, the veil of the temple was torn in two from top to bottom; and the earth quaked, and the rocks were split."

Manuscript Releases, **Vol. 12, p. 409**
"When Christ cried, 'It is finished,' God's unseen hand rent the strong fabric composing

the veil of the Temple from top to bottom. The way into the Holiest of all was made manifest. God bowed His head satisfied. Now His justice and mercy could blend. He could be just, and yet the justifier of all who should believe on Christ. He looked upon the victim expiring on the cross, and said, 'It is finished. The human race shall have another trial.' The redemption price was paid, and Satan fell like lightning from heaven."

The Youth's Instructor, April 25, 1901

"Entire justice was done in the atonement. In the place of the sinner, the spotless Son of God received the penalty, and the sinner goes free as long as he receives and holds Christ as his personal Saviour. Though guilty, he is looked upon as innocent. Christ fulfilled every requirement demanded by justice. God's character as a God of holiness, a God of goodness, compassion, and love combined, was revealed in his Son. In the cross of Christ, God gave the world a mighty pledge of his justice and love."

Revelation 3:7

"And to the angel of the church in Philadelphia write, 'These things says He who is holy, He who is true, "He who has the key of David, He who opens and no one shuts, and shuts and no one opens." ' "

John 19:28

"After this, Jesus, knowing that all things were now accomplished, that the Scripture might be fulfilled, said, 'I thirst!' "

Manuscript Releases, vol. 12, pp. 408, 409

" 'Jesus, knowing that all things were now accomplished [John 19:28],' cried out with a loud voice, 'It is finished.' The work that Thou gavest Me is accomplished. Thus He gave His dying testimony to men and angels that the work He came to earth to do was to save a perishing world by His death.

"When Christ spoke these words, He addressed His Father. Christ was not alone in making this great sacrifice. It was the fulfillment of the covenant made between the Father and the Son before the foundation of the earth was laid. With clasped hands they entered into the solemn pledge that Christ would become the substitute and surety for the human race if they were overcome by Satan's sophistry. The compact was now being fully consummated. The climax was reached. Christ had the consciousness that He had fulfilled to the letter the pledge He had made. In death He was more than conqueror. The redemption price has been paid. His right hand and His glorious holy arm have gotten Him the victory.

"When He uttered the cry, 'It is finished,' Christ knew that the battle was won. As a moral conqueror, He planted His banner on the eternal heights. Was there not joy among the angels? Not a son, not a daughter of Adam, but could now lay hold on the merits of the spotless Son of God, and say, Christ has died for me. He is my Saviour. The blood that speaketh better things than that of Abel has been shed.

"The darkness rolled away from the Saviour and from the cross. Christ bowed His head and died. In His incarnation He had reached the prescribed limit as a sacrifice, but not as a Redeemer. The controversy in regard to the rebellion was answered. The human race has an open door set before them. 'These things saith He that is holy, He that is true, He that hath the key of David, He that openeth, and no man shutteth; and shutteth, and no man openeth' [Revelation 3:7]. "

The Daily Service in the Sanctuary on Earth

Leviticus 4:28–31

"Or if his sin which he has committed comes to his knowledge, then he shall bring as his offering a kid of the goats, a female without blemish, for his sin which he has committed. And he shall lay his hand on the head of the sin offering, and kill the sin offering at the place of the burnt offering. Then the priest shall take *some* of its blood with his finger, put *it* on the horns of the altar of burnt offering, and pour all *the remaining* blood at the base of the altar. He shall remove all its fat, as fat is removed from the sacrifice of the peace offering; and the priest shall burn it on the altar for a sweet aroma to the Lord. So the priest shall make atonement for him, and it shall be forgiven him."

Patriarchs and Prophets, **p. 353**

"The incense, ascending with the prayers of Israel, represents the merits and intercession of Christ, His perfect righteousness, which through faith is imputed to His people, and which can alone make the worship of sinful beings acceptable to God. Before the veil of the most holy place was an altar of perpetual intercession, before the holy, an altar of continual atonement. By blood and by incense God was to be approached—symbols pointing to the great Mediator, through whom sinners may approach Jehovah, and through whom alone mercy and salvation can be granted to the repentant, believing soul."

Manuscript 14, **1901**

"In the service of the Jewish priesthood we are continually reminded of the sacrifice and intercession of Christ. *All who come to Christ today are to remember that His merit is the*

incense that mingles with the prayers of those who repent of their sins and receive pardon and mercy and grace. *Our need of Christ's intercession is constant."*

Patriarchs and Prophets, **p. 354**

"The most important part of the daily ministration was the service performed in behalf of individuals. The repentant sinner brought his offering to the door of the tabernacle, and, placing his hand upon the victim's head, confessed his sins, thus in figure transferring them from himself to the innocent sacrifice. By his own hand the animal was then slain, and the blood was carried by the priest into the holy place and sprinkled before the veil, behind which was the ark containing the law that the sinner had transgressed. By this ceremony the sin was, through the blood, transferred in figure to the sanctuary."

Hebrews 9:22

"And according to the law almost all things are purified with blood, and without shedding of blood there is no remission."

Leviticus 17:11

"For the life of the flesh *is* in the blood, and I have given it to you upon the altar to make atonement for your souls; for it *is* the blood *that* makes atonement for the soul."

The Great Controversy, **p. 418**

"The ministration of the earthly sanctuary consisted of two divisions; the priests ministered daily in the holy place, while once a year the high priest performed a special work of atonement in the most holy, for the cleansing of the sanctuary. Day by day the repentant sinner brought his offering to the door of the tabernacle and, placing his hand upon the victim's head, confessed his sins, thus in figure transferring them from himself to the innocent sacrifice. The animal was then slain. 'Without shedding of blood [Hebrews 9:22],' says the apostle, there is no remission of sin. 'The life of the flesh is in the blood.' Leviticus 17:11. The broken law of God demanded the life of the transgressor. The blood, representing the forfeited life of the sinner, whose guilt the victim bore, was carried by the priest into the holy place and sprinkled before the veil, behind which was the ark containing the law that the sinner had transgressed. By this ceremony the sin was, through the blood, transferred in figure to the sanctuary."

The Day of Atonement Service in the Sanctuary on Earth

Leviticus 16:8, 15–19, 21, 22, 32–34

" 'Then Aaron shall cast lots for the two goats: one lot for the Lord and the other lot for the scapegoat.'

'Then he shall kill the goat of the sin offering, which *is* for the people, bring its blood inside the veil, do with that blood as he did with the blood of the bull, and sprinkle it on the mercy seat and before the mercy seat. So he shall make atonement for the Holy *Place*, because of the uncleanness of the children of Israel, and because of their transgressions, for all their sins; and so he shall do for the tabernacle of meeting which remains among them in the midst of their uncleanness. There shall be no man in the tabernacle of meeting when he goes in to make atonement in the Holy *Place*, until he comes out, that he may make atonement for himself, for his household, and for all the assembly of Israel. And he shall go out to the altar that *is* before the Lord, and make atonement for it, and shall take some of the blood of the bull and some of the blood of the goat, and put it on the horns of the altar

all around. Then he shall sprinkle some of the blood on it with his finger seven times, cleanse it, and consecrate it from the uncleanness of the children of Israel.'

'Aaron shall lay both his hands on the head of the live goat, confess over it all the iniquities of the children of Israel, and all their transgressions, concerning all their sins, putting them on the head of the goat, and shall send *it* away into the wilderness by the hand of a suitable man. The goat shall bear on itself all their iniquities to an uninhabited land; and he shall release the goat in the wilderness.'

'And the priest, who is anointed and consecrated to minister as priest in his father's place, shall make atonement, and put on the linen clothes, the holy garments; then he shall make atonement for the Holy Sanctuary, and he shall make atonement for the tabernacle of meeting and for the altar, and he shall make atonement for the priests and for all the people of the assembly. This shall be an everlasting statute for you, to make atonement for the children of Israel, for all their sins, once a year.' And he did as the Lord commanded Moses."

The Great Controversy, pp. 418, 419

"Such was the work that went on, day by day, throughout the year. The sins of Israel were thus transferred to the sanctuary, and a special work became necessary for their removal. God commanded that an atonement be made for each of the sacred apartments. 'He shall make an atonement for the holy place, because of the uncleanness of the children of Israel, and because of their transgressions in all their sins: and so shall he do for the tabernacle of the congregation, that remaineth among them in the midst of their uncleanness.' An atonement was also to be made for the altar, to 'cleanse it, and hallow it from the uncleanness of the children of Israel.' Leviticus 16:16, 19.

"Once a year, on the great Day of Atonement, the priest entered the most holy place for the cleansing of the sanctuary. The work there performed completed the yearly round of ministration. On the Day of Atonement two kids of the goats were brought to the door of the tabernacle, and lots were cast upon them, 'one lot for the Lord, and the other lot for the scapegoat.' Verse 8. The goat upon which fell the lot for the Lord was to be slain as a sin offering for the people. And the priest was to bring his blood within the veil and sprinkle it upon the mercy seat and before the mercy seat. The blood was also to be sprinkled upon the altar of incense that was before the veil.

" 'And Aaron shall lay both his hands upon the head of the live goat, and confess over him all the iniquities of the children of Israel, and all their transgressions in all their sins, putting them upon the head of the goat, and shall send him away by the hand of a fit man into the wilderness: and the goat shall bear upon him all their iniquities unto a land not inhabited.' Verses 21, 22. The scapegoat came no more into the camp of Israel, and the man who led him away was required to wash himself and his clothing with water before returning to the camp."

Hebrews 8:5

"Who serve the copy and shadow of the heavenly things, as Moses was divinely instructed when he was about to make the tabernacle. For He said, 'See *that* you make all things according to the pattern shown you on the mountain.' "

The Great Controversy, p. 420

"Important truths concerning the atonement are taught by the typical service. A substitute was accepted in the sinner's stead; but the sin was not canceled by the blood of the victim. A means was thus provided by which it was transferred to the sanctuary. By the offering of blood the sinner acknowledged the authority of the law, confessed his guilt in transgression, and expressed his desire for pardon through faith in a Redeemer to come; but he was not yet entirely released from the condemnation of the law. On the Day of Atonement the high priest, having taken an offering from the congregation, went into the most holy place with the blood of this offering, and sprinkled it upon the mercy seat, directly over the law, to make satisfaction for its claims. Then, in his character of mediator, he took the sins upon himself and bore them from the sanctuary. Placing his hands upon the head of the scapegoat, he confessed over him all these sins, thus in figure transferring them from himself to the goat. The goat then bore them away, and they were regarded as forever separated from the people.

"Such was the service performed 'unto the example and shadow of heavenly things [Hebrews 8:5].' And what was done in type in the ministration of the earthly sanctuary is done in reality in the ministration of the heavenly sanctuary."

The Daily Service in the Sanctuary in Heaven

Revelation 4:5

"And from the throne proceeded lightnings, thunderings, and voices. Seven lamps of fire *were* burning before the throne, which are the seven Spirits of God."

Revelation 8:3

"Then another angel, having a golden censer, came and stood at the altar. He was given much incense, that he should offer *it* with the prayers of all the saints upon the golden altar which was before the throne."

The Great Controversy, pp. 414, 415

"The holy places of the sanctuary in heaven are represented by the two apartments in the sanctuary on earth. As in vision the apostle John was granted a view of the temple of God in heaven, he beheld there 'seven lamps of fire burning before the throne.' Revelation 4:5. He saw an angel 'having a golden censer; and there was given unto him much incense, that he should offer it with the prayers of all saints upon the golden altar which was before the throne.' Revelation 8:3. Here the prophet was permitted to behold the first apartment of the sanctuary in heaven; and he saw there the 'seven lamps of fire' and 'the golden altar,' represented by the golden candlestick and the altar of incense in the sanctuary on earth."

Hebrews 6:19, 20

"This *hope* we have as an anchor of the soul, both sure and steadfast, and which enters the *Presence* behind the veil, where the forerunner has entered for us, *even* Jesus, having become High Priest forever according to the order of Melchizedek."

The Great Controversy, p. 489

"The intercession of Christ in man's behalf in the sanctuary above is as essential to the plan of salvation as was His death upon the cross. By His death He began that work which after His resurrection He ascended to complete in heaven. We must by faith enter within the veil, 'whither the forerunner is for us entered.' Hebrews 6:20. There the light from the cross of Calvary is reflected. There we may gain a clearer insight into the mysteries of redemption. The salvation of man is accomplished at an infinite expense to heaven; the sacrifice made is equal to the broadest demands of the broken law of God. Jesus has opened the way to the Father's throne, and through His mediation the sincere desire of all who come to Him in faith may be presented before God."

> "The intercession of Christ in man's behalf in the sanctuary above is as essential to the plan of salvation as was His death upon the cross."

Hebrews 9:24

"For Christ has not entered the holy places made with hands, *which are* copies of the true, but into heaven itself, now to appear in the presence of God for us."

Hebrews 9:12

"Not with the blood of goats and calves, but with His own blood He entered the Most Holy Place once for all, having obtained eternal redemption."

Zechariah 6:12, 13

"Then speak to him, saying, 'Thus says the Lord of hosts, saying: "Behold, the Man whose name *is* the BRANCH! From His place He shall branch out, and He shall build the temple of the Lord; Yes, He shall build the temple of the Lord. He shall bear the glory, and shall sit and rule on His throne; so He shall be a priest on His throne, and the counsel of peace shall be between them both." ' "

Ephesians 2:20–22

"Having been built on the foundation of the apostles and prophets, Jesus Christ Himself being the chief *cornerstone*, in whom the whole building, being fitted together, grows into a holy temple in the Lord, in whom you also are being built together for a dwelling place of God in the Spirit."

Revelation 1:5, 6

"And from Jesus Christ, the faithful witness, the firstborn from the dead, and the ruler over the kings of the earth. To Him who loved us and washed us from our sins in His own blood, and has made us kings and priests to His God and Father, to Him *be* glory and dominion forever and ever. Amen."

Luke 1:32, 33

"He will be great, and will be called the Son of the Highest; and the Lord God will give Him the throne of His father David. And He will reign over the house of Jacob forever, and of His kingdom there will be no end."

Revelation 3:21

"To him who overcomes I will grant to sit with Me on My throne, as I also overcame and sat down with My Father on His throne."

Isaiah 53:4

"Surely He has borne our griefs and carried our sorrows; yet we esteemed Him stricken, smitten by God, and afflicted."

Hebrews 4:15

"For we do not have a High Priest who cannot sympathize with our weaknesses, but was in all *points* tempted as *we are, yet* without sin."

Hebrews 2:18

"For in that He Himself has suffered, being tempted, He is able to aid those who are tempted."

1 John 2:1

"My little children, these things I write to you, so that you may not sin. And if anyone sins, we have an Advocate with the Father, Jesus Christ the righteous."

John 16:26, 27

"In that day you will ask in My name, and I do not say to you that I shall pray the Father for you; for the Father Himself loves you, because you have loved Me, and have believed that I came forth from God."

***The Great Controversy*, pp. 415–417**

"The work of Christ as man's intercessor is presented in that beautiful prophecy of Zechariah concerning Him 'whose name is the Branch.' Says the prophet: 'He shall build the temple of the Lord; and He shall bear the glory, and shall sit and rule upon His [the Father's] throne: and He shall be a priest upon His throne: and the *counsel of peace* shall be between Them both.' Zechariah 6:12, 13.

" 'He shall build the temple of the Lord.' By His sacrifice and mediation Christ is both the foundation and the builder of the church of God. The apostle Paul points to Him as 'the chief Cornerstone; in whom all the building fitly framed together groweth into an holy temple in the Lord: in whom ye also,' he says, 'are builded together for an habitation of God through the Spirit.' Ephesians 2:20–22.

" 'He shall bear the glory.' To Christ belongs the glory of redemption for the fallen race. Through the eternal ages, the song of the ransomed ones will be: 'Unto Him that loved us, and washed us from our sins in His own blood, . . . to Him be glory and dominion for ever and ever.' Revelation 1:5, 6.

"He 'shall sit and rule upon His throne; and He shall be a priest upon His throne [Zechariah 6:13].' Not now 'upon the throne of His glory;' the kingdom of glory has not yet been ushered in. Not until His work as a mediator shall be ended will God 'give unto Him the throne of His father David,' a kingdom of which 'there shall be no end.' Luke 1:32, 33. As a priest, Christ is now set down with the Father in His throne. Revelation 3:21. Upon the throne with the eternal, self-existent One is He who 'hath borne our griefs, and carried our sorrows,' who 'was in all points tempted like as we are, yet without sin,' that He might be 'able to succor them that are tempted.' 'If any man sin, we have an advocate with the Father.' Isaiah 53:4; Hebrews 4:15; 2:18; 1 John 2:1. His intercession is that of a pierced and broken body, of a spotless life. The wounded hands, the pierced side, the marred feet, plead for fallen man, whose redemption was purchased at such infinite cost.

" 'And the counsel of peace shall be between Them both.' The love of the Father, no less than of the Son, is the fountain of salvation for the lost race. Said Jesus to His disciples before He went away: 'I say not unto you, that I will pray the Father for you: for the Father Himself loveth you.' John 16:26, 27. God was 'in Christ, reconciling the world unto Himself.' 2 Corinthians 5:19. And in the ministration in the sanctuary above, 'the counsel of peace shall be between Them both.' 'God *so loved* the world, that He gave His only-begotten Son, that whosoever believeth in Him should not perish, but have everlasting life.' John 3:16."

Acts 1:9–11
"Now when He had spoken these things, while they watched, He was taken up, and a cloud received Him out of their sight. And while they looked steadfastly toward heaven as He went up, behold, two men stood by them in white apparel, who also said, 'Men of Galilee, why do you stand gazing up into heaven? This *same* Jesus, who was taken up from you into heaven, will so come in like manner as you saw Him go into heaven.' "

The Desire of Ages, **pp. 831, 832**
"While the disciples were still gazing upward, voices addressed them which sounded like richest music. They turned, and saw two angels in the form of men, who spoke to them, saying, 'Ye men of Galilee, why stand ye gazing up into heaven? this same Jesus, which is taken up from you into heaven, shall so come in like manner as ye have seen Him go into heaven.' "

Psalm 24:7
"Lift up your heads, O you gates! And be lifted up, you everlasting doors! And the King of glory shall come in."

The Desire of Ages, **pp. 833, 834**
"All heaven was waiting to welcome the Saviour to the celestial courts. As He ascended, He led the way, and the multitude of captives set free at His resurrection followed. The heavenly host, with shouts and acclamations of praise and celestial song, attended the joyous train.

"As they drew near to the city of God, the challenge is given by the escorting angels,—'Lift up your heads, O ye gates; and be ye lift up, ye everlasting doors; and the King of glory shall come in [Psalm 124:7].' …

"Then the portals of the city of God are opened wide, and the angelic throng sweep through the gates amid a burst of rapturous music.

"There is the throne, and around it the rainbow of promise. There are cherubim and seraphim. The commanders of the angel hosts, the sons of God, the representatives of the unfallen worlds, are assembled. The heavenly council before which Lucifer had accused God and His Son, the representatives of those sinless realms over which Satan had thought to establish his dominion,—all are there to welcome the Redeemer. They are eager to celebrate His triumph and to glorify their King.

"But He waves them back. Not yet; He cannot now receive the coronet of glory and the royal robe. He enters into the presence of His Father [Revelation 5:6]. He points to His wounded head, the pierced side, the marred feet; He lifts His hands, bearing the print of nails.… Before the foundations of the earth were laid, the Father and the Son had united in a covenant to redeem man if he should be overcome by Satan. They had clasped Their hands in a solemn pledge that Christ should become the surety for the human race. This pledge Christ has fulfilled. When upon the cross He cried out, 'It is finished,' He addressed the Father. The compact had been fully carried out.…

"The voice of God is heard proclaiming that justice is satisfied."

Hebrews 1:6
"But when He again brings the firstborn into the world, He says: 'Let all the angels of God worship Him.' "

The Desire of Ages, p. 834
"The Father's arms encircle His Son, and the word is given, 'Let all the angels of God worship Him.' Hebrews 1:6.

"With joy unutterable, rulers and principalities and powers acknowledge the supremacy of the Prince of life. The angel host prostrate themselves before Him, while the glad shout fills all the courts of heaven."

Revelation 5:12, 13
"Saying with a loud voice: 'Worthy is the Lamb who was slain to receive power and riches and wisdom, and strength and honor and glory and blessing!' And every creature which is in heaven and on the earth and under the earth and such as are in the sea, and all that are in them, I heard saying: 'Blessing and honor and glory and power *be* to Him who sits on the throne, and to the Lamb, forever and ever!' "

Isaiah 13:12
"I will make a mortal more rare than fine gold, a man more than the golden wedge of Ophir."

The Desire of Ages, p. 790
"Jesus refused to receive the homage of His people until He had the assurance that His sacrifice was accepted by the Father. He ascended to the heavenly courts, and from God Himself heard the assurance that His atonement for the sins of men had been ample, that through His blood all might gain eternal life. The Father ratified the covenant made with Christ, that He would receive repentant and obedient men, and would love them even as He loves His Son. Christ was to complete His work, and fulfill His pledge to 'make a man more precious than fine gold; even a man than the golden wedge of Ophir.' Isaiah 13:12."

John 20:17
"Jesus said to her, 'Do not cling to Me, for I have not yet ascended to My Father; but go to

My brethren and say to them, "I am ascending to My Father and your Father, and *to* My God and your God." ' "

"The Father ratified the covenant made with Christ, that He would receive repentant and obedient men, and would love them even as He loves His Son."

Hebrews 7:25
"Therefore He is also able to save to the uttermost those who come to God through Him, since He always lives to make intercession for them."

The Desire of Ages, p. 835
"From that scene of heavenly joy, there comes back to us on earth the echo of Christ's own wonderful words, 'I ascend unto My Father, and your Father; and to My God, and your God.' John 20:17.... 'Wherefore He is able also to save them to the uttermost that come unto God by Him, seeing He ever liveth to make intercession for them.' Hebrews 7:25."

Hebrews 9:11, 12
"But Christ came *as* High Priest of the good things to come, with the greater and more perfect tabernacle not made with hands, that is, not of this creation. Not with the blood of goats and calves, but with His own blood He entered the Most Holy Place once for all, having obtained eternal redemption."

The Great Controversy, pp. 420, 421
"After His ascension our Saviour began His work as our high priest. Says Paul: 'Christ is not entered into the holy places made with hands, which are the figures of the true; but into heaven itself, now to appear in the presence of God for us.' Hebrews 9:24.

"The ministration of the priest throughout the year in the first apartment of the sanctuary, 'within the veil' which formed the door and separated the holy place from the outer court, represents the work of ministration upon which Christ entered at His ascension. It was the work of the priest in the daily ministration to present before God the blood of the sin offering, also the incense which ascended with the prayers of Israel. So did Christ plead His blood before the Father in behalf of sinners, and present before Him also, with the precious fragrance of His own righteousness, the prayers of penitent believers. Such was the work of ministration in the first apartment of the sanctuary in heaven.

"Thither the faith of Christ's disciples followed Him as He ascended from their sight. Here their hopes centered, 'which hope we have,' said Paul, 'as an anchor of the soul, both sure and steadfast, and which entereth into that within the veil; whither the forerunner is for us entered, even Jesus, made an high priest forever.' 'Neither by the blood of goats and calves, but by His own blood He entered in once into the holy place, having obtained eternal redemption for us.' Hebrews 6:19, 20; 9:12.

"For eighteen centuries this work of ministration continued in the first apartment of the sanctuary. The blood of Christ, pleaded in behalf of penitent believers, secured their pardon and acceptance with the Father, yet their sins still remained upon the books of record. As in the typical service there was a work of atonement at the close of the year, so before Christ's work for the redemption of men is completed there is a work of atonement for the removal of sin from the sanctuary. This is the service which began when the 2300 days ended. At that time, as foretold by Daniel the prophet, our High Priest entered the most holy, to perform the last division of His solemn work—to cleanse the sanctuary."

Ephesians 2:13, 14
"But now in Christ Jesus you who once were far off have been brought near by the blood of Christ. For He Himself is our peace, who has made both one, and has broken down the middle wall of separation."

Hebrews 10:11, 12
"And every priest stands ministering daily and offering repeatedly the same sacrifices, which can never take away sins. But this Man, after He had offered one sacrifice for sins forever, sat down at the right hand of God."

The Day of Atonement Service in the Sanctuary in Heaven
The Judgment / The Investigative Phase / (See "The Three Angels' Messages")

1 Peter 4:17
"For the time *has come* for judgment to begin at the house of God; and if *it begins* with us first, what will *be* the end of those who do not obey the gospel of God?"

Daniel 7:9, 10, 13
"I watched till thrones were put in place, and the Ancient of Days was seated; His garment *was* white as snow, and the hair of His head *was* like pure wool. His throne *was* a fiery flame, its wheels a burning fire; a fiery stream issued and came forth from before Him. A thousand thousands ministered to Him; ten thousand times ten thousand stood before

Him. The court was seated, and the books were opened."

"I was watching in the night visions, and behold, *One* like the Son of Man, coming with the clouds of heaven! He came to the Ancient of Days, and they brought Him near before Him."

Revelation 20:12
"And I saw the dead, small and great, standing before God, and books were opened. And another book was opened, which is *the Book* of Life. And the dead were judged according to their works, by the things which were written in the books."

Luke 10:20
"Nevertheless do not rejoice in this, that the spirits are subject to you, but rather rejoice because your names are written in heaven."

Philippians 4:3
"And I urge you also, true companion, help these women who labored with me in the gospel, with Clement also, and the rest of my fellow workers, whose names *are* in the Book of Life."

Daniel 12:1
"At that time Michael shall stand up, the great prince who stands *watch* over the sons of your people; and there shall be a time of trouble, such as never was since there was a nation, *even* to that time. And at that time your people shall be delivered, every one who is found written in the book."

Revelation 21:27
"But there shall by no means enter it anything that defiles, or causes an abomination or a lie, but only those who are written in the Lamb's Book of Life."

Malachi 3:16

"Then those who feared the Lord spoke to one another, and the Lord listened and heard them; so a book of remembrance was written before Him for those who fear the Lord and who meditate on His name."

Nehemiah 13:14

"Remember me, O my God, concerning this, and do not wipe out my good deeds that I have done for the house of my God, and for its services!"

Psalm 56:8

"You number my wanderings; put my tears into Your bottle; *are they* not in Your book?"

Ecclesiastes 12:14

"For God will bring every work into judgment, including every secret thing, whether good or evil."

Matthew 12:36, 37

"But I say to you that for every idle word men may speak, they will give account of it in the day of judgment. For by your words you will be justified, and by your words you will be condemned."

1 Corinthians 4:5

"Therefore judge nothing before the time, until the Lord comes, who will both bring to light the hidden things of darkness and reveal the counsels of the hearts. Then each one's praise will come from God."

Isaiah 65:6, 7

" 'Behold, *it is* written before Me: I will not keep silence, but will repay—even repay into their bosom—Your iniquities and the iniquities of your fathers together,' says the Lord, 'Who have burned incense on the mountains and blasphemed Me on the hills; therefore I will measure their former work into their bosom.' "

Luke 20:35, 36

"But those who are counted worthy to attain that age, and the resurrection from the dead, neither marry nor are given in marriage; nor can they die anymore, for they are equal to the angels and are sons of God, being sons of the resurrection."

John 5:29

"And come forth—those who have done good, to the resurrection of life, and those who have done evil, to the resurrection of condemnation."

Exodus 32:33

"And the Lord said to Moses, 'Whoever has sinned against Me, I will blot him out of My book.' "

Ezekiel 18:24

"But when a righteous man turns away from his righteousness and commits iniquity, and does according to all the abominations that the wicked *man* does, shall he live? All the righteousness which he has done shall not be remembered; because of the unfaithfulness of which he is guilty and the sin which he has committed, because of them he shall die."

Isaiah 43:25

"I, *even* I, *am* He who blots out your transgressions for My own sake; and I will not remember your sins."

Revelation 3:3–5

"Remember therefore how you have received and heard; hold fast and repent. Therefore if you will not watch, I will come upon you as a thief, and you will not know what hour I will come upon you. You have a few names even in Sardis who have not defiled their garments; and they shall walk with Me in white, for they are worthy. He who overcomes shall be clothed in white garments, and I will not blot out his name from the Book of Life; but I will confess his name before My Father and before His angels."

Matthew 10:32, 33

"Therefore whoever confesses Me before men, him I will also confess before My Father who is in heaven. But whoever denies Me before men, him I will also deny before My Father who is in heaven."

Micah 4:8

"And you, O tower of the flock, the stronghold of the daughter of Zion, to you shall it come, even the former dominion shall come, the kingdom of the daughter of Jerusalem."

Psalm 51:17

"The sacrifices of God *are* a broken spirit, a broken and a contrite heart—these, O God, You will not despise."

Zechariah 3:2

"And the Lord said to Satan, 'The Lord rebuke you, Satan! The Lord who has chosen Jerusalem rebuke you! *Is* this not a brand plucked from the fire?' "

Ephesians 5:27

"That He might present her to Himself a glorious church, not having spot or wrinkle or any such thing, but that she should be holy and without blemish."

Acts 3:19, 20

"Repent therefore and be converted, that your sins may be blotted out, so that times of refreshing may come from the presence of the Lord, and that He may send Jesus Christ, who was preached to you before."

Hebrews 9:28

"So Christ was offered once to bear the sins of many. To those who eagerly wait for Him He will appear a second time, apart from sin, for salvation."

Proverbs 28:13

"He who covers his sins will not prosper, but whoever confesses and forsakes *them* will have mercy."

2 Corinthians 12:9

"And He said to me, 'My grace is sufficient for you, for My strength is made perfect in weakness.' Therefore most gladly I will rather boast in my infirmities, that the power of Christ may rest upon me."

Matthew 11:29, 30

"Take My yoke upon you and learn from Me, for I am gentle and lowly in heart, and you will find rest for your souls. For My yoke *is* easy and My burden is light."

Mark 13:33, 35, 36

"Take heed, watch and pray; for you do not know when the time is…. Watch therefore, for you do not know when the master of the house is coming—in the evening, at midnight, at the crowing of the rooster, or in the morning—lest, coming suddenly, he find you sleeping."

Revelation 22:11, 12

"He who is unjust, let him be unjust still; he who is filthy, let him be filthy still; he who is righteous, let him be righteous still; he who is holy, let him be holy still. And behold, I am coming quickly, and My reward *is* with Me, to give to every one according to his work."

Matthew 24:39

"And did not know until the flood came and took them all away, so also will the coming of the Son of Man be."

Daniel 5:27

"TEKEL: You have been weighed in the balances, and found wanting."

The Great Controversy, pp. 480–491

"In the typical service only those who had come before God with confession and repentance, and whose sins, through the blood of the sin offering, were transferred to the sanctuary, had a part in the service of the Day of Atonement. So in the great day of final atonement and investigative judgment the only cases considered are those of the professed people of God. The judgment of the wicked is a distinct and separate work, and takes place at a later period. 'Judgment must begin at the house of God: and if it first begin at us, what shall the end be of them that obey not the gospel?' 1 Peter 4:17.

"The books of record in heaven, in which the names and the deeds of men are registered, are to determine the decisions of the judgment. Says the prophet Daniel: 'The judgment was set, and the books were opened [Daniel 7:10].' The revelator, describing the same scene, adds: 'Another book was opened, which is the book of life: and the dead were judged out of those things which were written in the books, according to their works.' Revelation 20:12.

"The book of life contains the names of all who have ever entered the service of God.

Jesus bade His disciples: 'Rejoice, because your names are written in heaven.' Luke 10:20. Paul speaks of his faithful fellow workers, 'whose names are in the book of life.' Philippians 4:3. Daniel, looking down to 'a time of trouble, such as never was,' declares that God's people shall be delivered, 'everyone that shall be found written in the book.' And the revelator says that those only shall enter the city of God whose names 'are written in the Lamb's book of life.' Daniel 12:1; Revelation 21:27.

" 'A book of remembrance' is written before God, in which are recorded the good deeds of 'them that feared the Lord, and that thought upon His name.' Malachi 3:16. Their words of faith, their acts of love, are registered in heaven. Nehemiah refers to this when he says: 'Remember me, O my God, … and wipe not out my good deeds that I have done for the house of my God.' Nehemiah 13:14. In the book of God's remembrance every deed of righteousness is immortalized. There every temptation resisted, every evil overcome, every word of tender pity expressed, is faithfully chronicled. And every act of sacrifice, every suffering and sorrow endured for Christ's sake, is recorded. Says the psalmist: 'Thou tellest my wanderings: put Thou my tears into Thy bottle: are they not in Thy book?' Psalm 56:8.

"There is a record also of the sins of men. 'For God shall bring every work into judgment, with every secret thing, whether it be good, or whether it be evil.' 'Every idle word that men shall speak, they shall give account thereof in the day of judgment.' Says the Saviour: 'By thy words thou shalt be justified, and by thy words thou shalt be condemned.' Ecclesiastes 12:14; Matthew 12:36, 37. The secret purposes and motives appear in the unerring register; for God 'will bring to light the hidden things of darkness, and will make manifest the counsels of the hearts.' 1 Corinthians 4:5. 'Behold, it is written before Me, ... your iniquities, and the iniquities of your fathers together, saith the Lord.' Isaiah 65:6, 7.

"Every man's work passes in review before God and is registered for faithfulness or unfaithfulness. Opposite each name in the books of heaven is entered with terrible exactness every wrong word, every selfish act, every unfulfilled duty, and every secret sin, with every artful dissembling. Heaven-sent warnings or reproofs neglected, wasted moments, unimproved opportunities, the influence exerted for good or for evil, with its far-reaching results, all are chronicled by the recording angel....

"Those who in the judgment are 'accounted worthy' will have a part in the resurrection of the just. Jesus said: 'They which shall be accounted worthy to obtain that world, and the resurrection from the dead, ... are equal unto the angels; and are the children of God, being the children of the resurrection.' Luke 20:35, 36. And again He declares that 'they that have done good' shall come forth 'unto the resurrection of life.' John 5:29. The righteous dead will not be raised until after the judgment at which they are accounted worthy of 'the resurrection of life.' Hence they will not be present in person at the tribunal when their records are examined and their cases decided.

"Jesus will appear as their advocate, to plead in their behalf before God. 'If any man sin, we have an advocate with the Father, Jesus Christ the righteous.' 1 John 2:1. 'For Christ is not entered into the holy places made with hands, which are the figures of the true; but into heaven itself, now to appear in the presence of God for us.' 'Wherefore He is able also to save them to the uttermost that come unto God by Him, seeing He ever liveth to make intercession for them.' Hebrews 9:24; 7:25.

"As the books of record are opened in the judgment, the lives of all who have believed on Jesus come in review before God. Beginning with those who first lived upon the earth, our Advocate presents the cases of each successive generation, and closes with the living. Every name is mentioned, every case closely investigated. Names are accepted, names rejected. When any have sins remaining upon the books of record, unrepented of and unforgiven, their names will be blotted out of the book of life, and the record of their good deeds will be erased from the book of God's remembrance. The Lord declared to Moses: 'Whosoever hath sinned against Me, him will I blot out of My book.' Exodus 32:33. And says the prophet Ezekiel: 'When the righteous turneth away from his righteousness, and committeth iniquity, ... all his righteousness that he hath done shall not be mentioned.' Ezekiel 18:24.

"All who have truly repented of sin, and by faith claimed the blood of Christ as their atoning sacrifice, have had pardon entered against their names in the books of heaven; as they have become partakers of the righteousness of Christ, and their characters are found to be in harmony with the law of God, their sins will be blotted out, and they themselves will be accounted worthy of eternal life. The Lord declares, by the prophet Isaiah: 'I, even I, am He that blotteth out thy transgressions for Mine own sake, and will not remember thy sins.' Isaiah 43:25. Said Jesus: 'He that overcometh, the same shall be clothed in white raiment; and I will not blot out his name out of the book of life, but I will confess his name before My Father, and before His angels.' 'Whosoever therefore shall confess Me before men, him will I confess also before My Father which is in heaven. But whosoever shall deny

Me before men, him will I also deny before My Father which is in heaven.' Revelation 3:5; Matthew 10:32, 33.

"The deepest interest manifested among men in the decisions of earthly tribunals but faintly represents the interest evinced in the heavenly courts when the names entered in the book of life come up in review before the Judge of all the earth. The divine Intercessor presents the plea that all who have overcome through faith in His blood be forgiven their transgressions, that they be restored to their Eden home, and crowned as joint heirs with Himself to 'the first dominion.' Micah 4:8. Satan in his efforts to deceive and tempt our race had thought to frustrate the divine plan in man's creation; but Christ now asks that this plan be carried into effect as if man had never fallen. He asks for His people not only pardon and justification, full and complete, but a share in His glory and a seat upon His throne....

"Jesus does not excuse their sins, but shows their penitence and faith, and, claiming for them forgiveness, He lifts His wounded hands before the Father and the holy angels, saying: I know them by name. I have graven them on the palms of My hands. 'The sacrifices of God are a broken spirit: a broken and a contrite heart, O God, Thou wilt not despise.' Psalm 51:17. And to the accuser of His people He declares: 'The Lord rebuke thee, O Satan; even the Lord that hath chosen Jerusalem rebuke thee: is not this a brand pluckcd out of the fire?' Zechariah 3:2. Christ will clothe His faithful ones with His own righteousness, that He may present them to His Father 'a glorious church, not having spot, or wrinkle, or any such thing.' Ephesians 5:27. Their names stand enrolled in the book of life, and concerning them it is written: 'They shall walk with Me in white: for they are worthy.' Revelation 3:4....

"The work of the investigative judgment and the blotting out of sins is to be accomplished before the second advent of the Lord. Since the dead are to be judged out of the things written in the books, it is impossible that the sins of men should be blotted out until after the judgment at which their cases are to be investigated. But the apostle Peter distinctly states that the sins of believers will be blotted out 'when the times of refreshing shall come from the presence of the Lord; and He shall send Jesus Christ.' Acts 3:19, 20. When the investigative judgment closes, Christ will come, and His reward will be with Him to give to every man as his work shall be.

"In the typical service the high priest, having made the atonement for Israel, came forth and blessed the congregation. So Christ, at the close of His work as mediator, will appear, 'without sin unto salvation' (Hebrews 9:28), to bless His waiting people with eternal life. As the priest, in removing the sins from the sanctuary, confessed them upon the head of the scapegoat, so Christ will place all these sins upon Satan, the originator and instigator of sin. The scapegoat, bearing the sins of Israel, was sent away 'unto a land not inhabited' (Leviticus 16:22); so Satan, bearing the guilt of all the sins which he has caused God's people to commit, will be for a thousand years confined to the earth, which will then be desolate, without inhabitant, and he will at last suffer the full penalty of sin in the fires that shall destroy all the wicked. Thus the great plan of redemption will reach its accomplishment in the final eradication of sin and the deliverance of all who have been willing to renounce evil.

"At the time appointed for the judgment—the close of the 2300 days, in 1844—began the work of investigation and blotting out of sins. All who have ever taken upon themselves the name of Christ must pass its searching scrutiny.

Both the living and the dead are to be judged 'out of those things which were written in the books, according to their works [Revelation 20:12].'

"Sins that have not been repented of and forsaken will not be pardoned and blotted out of the books of record, but will stand to witness against the sinner in the day of God. He may have committed his evil deeds in the light of day or in the darkness of night; but they were open and manifest before Him with whom we have to do. Angels of God witnessed each sin and registered it in the unerring records. Sin may be concealed, denied, covered up from father, mother, wife, children, and associates; no one but the guilty actors may cherish the least suspicion of the wrong; but it is laid bare before the intelligences of heaven. The darkness of the darkest night, the secrecy of all deceptive arts, is not sufficient to veil one thought from the knowledge of the Eternal. God has an exact record of every unjust account and every unfair dealing. He is not deceived by appearances of piety. He makes no mistakes in His estimation of character. Men may be deceived by those who are corrupt in heart, but God pierces all disguises and reads the inner life.

"How solemn is the thought! Day after day, passing into eternity, bears its burden of records for the books of heaven. Words once spoken, deeds once done, can never be recalled. Angels have registered both the good and the evil. The mightiest conqueror upon the earth cannot call back the record of even a single day. Our acts, our words, even our most secret motives, all have their weight in deciding our destiny for weal or woe. Though they may be forgotten by us, they will bear their testimony to justify or condemn.

"As the features of the countenance are reproduced with unerring accuracy on the polished plate of the artist, so the character is faithfully delineated in the books above. Yet how little solicitude is felt concerning that record which is to meet the gaze of heavenly beings. Could the veil which separates the visible from the invisible world be swept back, and the children of men behold an angel recording every word and deed, which they must meet again in the judgment, how many words that are daily uttered would remain unspoken, how many deeds would remain undone.

"In the judgment the use made of every talent will be scrutinized. How have we employed the capital lent us of Heaven? Will the Lord at His coming receive His own with usury? Have we improved the powers entrusted us, in hand and heart and brain, to the glory of God and the blessing of the world? How have we used our time, our pen, our voice, our money, our influence? What have we done for Christ, in the person of the poor, the afflicted, the orphan, or the widow? God has made us the depositaries of His holy word; what have we done with the light and truth given us to make men wise unto salvation? No value is attached to a mere profession of faith in Christ; only the love which is shown by works is counted genuine. Yet it is love alone which in the sight of Heaven makes any act of value. Whatever is done from love, however small it may appear in the estimation of men, is accepted and rewarded of God.

"The hidden selfishness of men stands revealed in the books of heaven. There is the record of unfulfilled duties to their fellow men, of forgetfulness of the Saviour's claims. There they will see how often were given to Satan the time, thought, and strength that belonged to Christ. Sad is the record which angels bear to heaven. Intelligent beings, professed followers of Christ, are absorbed in the acquirement of worldly possessions or the enjoyment of earthly pleasures. Money, time, and strength are sacrificed for display and self-indulgence; but few are the moments devoted to prayer, to the searching of the Scriptures, to humiliation of soul and confession of sin....

"Those who would share the benefits of the Saviour's mediation should permit nothing to interfere with their duty to perfect holiness in the fear of God. The precious hours, instead of being given to pleasure, to display, or to gain seeking, should be devoted to an earnest, prayerful study of the word of truth. The subject of the sanctuary and the investigative judgment should be clearly understood by the people of God. All need a knowledge for themselves of the position and work of their great High Priest. Otherwise it will be impossible for them to exercise the faith which is essential at this time or to occupy the position which God designs them to fill. Every individual has a soul to save or to lose. Each has a case pending at the bar of God. Each must meet the great Judge face to face. How important, then, that every mind contemplate often the solemn scene when the judgment shall sit and the books shall be opened, when, with Daniel, every individual must stand in his lot, at the end of the days.

"All who have received the light upon these subjects are to bear testimony of the great truths which God has committed to them. The sanctuary in heaven is the very center of Christ's work in behalf of men. It concerns every soul living upon the earth. It opens to view the plan of redemption, bringing us down to the very close of time and revealing the triumphant issue of the contest between righteousness and sin. It is of the utmost importance that all should thoroughly investigate these subjects and be able to give an answer to everyone that asketh them a reason of the hope that is in them.

"The intercession of Christ in man's behalf in the sanctuary above is as essential to the plan of salvation as was His death upon the cross. By His death He began that work which after His resurrection He ascended to complete in heaven. We must by faith enter within the veil, 'whither the forerunner is for us entered.' Hebrews 6:20. There the light from the cross of Calvary is reflected. There we may gain a clearer insight into the mysteries of redemption. The salvation of man is accomplished at an infinite expense to heaven; the sacrifice made is equal to the broadest demands of the broken law of God. Jesus has opened the way to the Father's throne, and through His mediation the sincere desire of all who come to Him in faith may be presented before God.

" 'He that covereth his sins shall not prosper: but whoso confesseth and forsaketh them shall have mercy.' Proverbs 28:13. If those who hide and excuse their faults could see how Satan exults over them, how he taunts Christ and holy angels with their course, they would make haste to confess their sins and to put them away. Through defects in the character, Satan works to gain control of the whole mind, and he knows that if these defects are cherished, he will succeed. Therefore he is constantly seeking to deceive the followers of Christ with his fatal sophistry that it is impossible for them to overcome. But Jesus pleads in their behalf His wounded hands, His bruised body; and He declares to all who would follow Him: 'My grace is sufficient for thee.' 2 Corinthians 12:9. 'Take My yoke upon you, and learn of Me; for I am meek and lowly in heart: and ye shall find rest unto your souls. For My yoke is easy, and My burden is light.' Matthew 11:29, 30. Let none, then, regard their defects as incurable. God will give faith and grace to overcome them.

"We are now living in the great day of atonement. In the typical service, while the high priest was making the atonement for Israel, all were required to afflict their souls by repentance of sin and humiliation before the Lord, lest they be cut off from among the people. In like manner, all who would have their names retained in the book of life should now, in the few remaining days of their probation, afflict their souls before God by sorrow for sin and true repentance. There must be deep, faithful searching of heart. The light, frivolous spirit indulged by so many professed Christians must be put away. There is earnest warfare before all who would subdue the evil tendencies that strive for the mastery. The work of preparation is an individual work. We are not saved in groups. The purity and devotion of one will not offset the want of these qualities in another. Though all nations are to pass in judgment before God, yet He will examine the case of each individual with as close and searching scrutiny as if there were not another being upon the earth. Everyone must be tested and found without spot or wrinkle or any such thing.

"Solemn are the scenes connected with the closing work of the atonement. Momentous are the interests involved therein. The judgment is now passing in the sanctuary above. For many years this work has been in progress. Soon—none know how soon—it will pass to the cases of the living. In the awful presence of God our lives are to come up in review. At this time above all others it behooves every soul to heed the Saviour's admonition: 'Watch and pray: for ye know not when the time is.' Mark 13:33. 'If therefore thou shalt not watch, I will come on thee as a thief, and thou shalt not know what hour I will come upon thee.' Revelation 3:3.

"When the work of the investigative judgment closes, the destiny of all will have been decided for life or death. Probation is ended a short time before the appearing of the Lord in the clouds of heaven. Christ in the Revelation, looking forward to that time, declares: 'He that is unjust, let him be unjust still: and he which is filthy, let him be filthy still: and he that is righteous let him be righteous still: and he that is holy, let him be holy still. And, behold, I come quickly; and My reward is with Me, to give every man according as his work shall be.' Revelation 22:11, 12.

"The righteous and the wicked will still be living upon the earth in their mortal state—men will be planting and building, eating and drinking, all unconscious that the final, irrevocable decision has been pronounced in the sanctuary above. Before the Flood, after Noah entered the ark, God shut him in and shut the ungodly out; but for seven days the people, knowing not that their doom was fixed, continued their careless, pleasure-loving life and mocked the warnings of impending judgment. 'So,' says the Saviour, 'shall also the coming of the Son of man be.' Matthew 24:39. Silently, unnoticed as the midnight thief, will come the decisive hour which marks the fixing of every man's destiny, the final withdrawal of mercy's offer to guilty men.

"When the work of the investigative judgment closes, the destiny of all will have been decided for life or death."

" 'Watch ye therefore: ... lest coming suddenly He find you sleeping.' Mark 13:35, 36. Perilous is the condition of those who, growing weary of their watch, turn to the attractions of the world. While the man of business is absorbed in the pursuit of gain, while the pleasure lover is seeking indulgence, while the daughter of fashion is arranging her adornments—it may be in that hour the Judge of all the earth will pronounce the sentence: 'Thou art weighed in the balances, and art found wanting.' Daniel 5:27."

The Second Coming of Jesus (The Battle of Armageddon)

Malachi 3:5

" 'And I will come near you for judgment; I will be a swift witness against sorcerers, against adulterers, against perjurers, against those who exploit wage earners and widows and orphans, and against those who turn away an alien— because they do not fear Me,' says the Lord of hosts."

Jude 14, 15

"Now Enoch, the seventh from Adam, prophesied about these men also, saying, 'Behold, the Lord comes with ten thousands of His saints, to execute judgment on all, to convict all who are ungodly among them of all their ungodly deeds which they have committed in an ungodly way, and of all the harsh things which ungodly sinners have spoken against Him.' "

The Great Controversy, pp. 425, 426

"Besides the coming of the Lord to His temple, Malachi also foretells His second advent, His coming for the execution of the judgment, in these words: 'And I will come near to you to judgment; and I will be a swift witness against the sorcerers, and against the adulterers, and against false swearers, and against those that oppress the hireling in his wages, the widow, and the fatherless, and that turn aside the stranger from his right, and fear not Me, saith the Lord of hosts.' Malachi 3:5. Jude refers to the same scene when he says, 'Behold, the Lord cometh with ten thousands of His saints, to execute judgment upon all, and to convince all that are ungodly among them of all their ungodly deeds.' Jude 14, 15. This coming, and the coming of the Lord to His temple, are distinct and separate events."

Revelation 19:11–21

"Now I saw heaven opened, and behold, a white horse. And He who sat on him *was* called Faithful and True, and in righteousness He judges and makes war. His eyes *were* like a flame of fire, and on His head *were* many crowns. He had a name written that no one knew except Himself. He *was* clothed with a robe dipped in blood, and His name is called The Word of God. And the armies in heaven, clothed in fine linen, white and clean, followed Him on white horses. Now out of His mouth goes a sharp sword, that with it He should strike the nations. And He Himself will rule them with a rod of iron. He Himself treads the winepress of the fierceness and wrath of Almighty God. And He has on *His* robe and on His thigh a name written: KING OF KINGS AND LORD OF LORDS.

"Then I saw an angel standing in the sun; and he cried with a loud voice, saying to all the birds that fly in the midst of heaven, 'Come and gather together for the supper of the great God, that you may eat the flesh of kings, the flesh of captains, the flesh of mighty men, the flesh of horses and of those who sit on them, and the flesh of all *people*, free and slave, both small and great.'

"And I saw the beast, the kings of the earth, and their armies, gathered together to make war against Him who sat on the horse and against His army. Then the beast was captured, and with him the false prophet who worked signs in his presence, by which he deceived those who received the mark of the beast and those who worshiped his image. These two were cast alive into the lake of fire burning with brimstone. And the rest were killed with the sword which proceeded from the mouth of Him who sat on the horse. And all the birds were filled with their flesh."

The Great Controversy, pp. 485, 486

"In the typical service the high priest, having made the atonement for Israel, came forth and blessed the congregation. So Christ, at the close of His work as mediator, will appear, 'without sin unto salvation' (Hebrews 9:28), to bless His waiting people with eternal life. As the priest, in removing the sins from the sanctuary, confessed them upon the head of the scapegoat, so Christ will place all these sins upon Satan, the originator and instigator of sin. The scapegoat, bearing the sins of Israel, was sent away 'unto a land not inhabited' (Leviticus 16:22); so Satan, bearing the guilt of all the sins which he has caused God's people to commit, will be for a thousand years confined to the earth, which will then be desolate, without inhabitant, and he will at last suffer the full penalty of sin in the fires that shall destroy all the wicked. Thus the great plan of redemption will reach its accomplishment in the final eradication of sin and the deliverance of all who have been willing to renounce evil."

Revelation 5:11

"Then I looked, and I heard the voice of many angels around the throne, the living creatures, and the elders; and the number of them was ten thousand times ten thousand, and thousands of thousands."

Habakkuk 3:3, 4

"God came from Teman, the Holy One from Mount Paran. *Selah*. His glory covered the heavens, and the earth was full of His praise. *His* brightness was like the light; He had rays *flashing* from His hand, and there His power *was* hidden."

Isaiah 53:3

"He is despised and rejected by men, a Man of sorrows and acquainted with grief. And we hid, as it were, *our* faces from Him; He was despised, and we did not esteem Him."

The Great Controversy, pp. 640, 641

"Soon there appears in the east a small black cloud, about half the size of a man's hand. It is the cloud which surrounds the Saviour and which seems in the distance to be shrouded in darkness. The people of God know this to be the sign of the Son of man. In solemn silence they gaze upon it as it draws nearer the earth, becoming lighter and more glorious, until it is a great white cloud, its base a glory like consuming fire, and above it the rainbow of the covenant. Jesus rides forth as a mighty conqueror. Not now a 'Man of Sorrows [Isaiah 53:3],' to drink the bitter cup of shame and woe, He comes, victor in heaven and earth, to judge the living and the dead. 'Faithful and True,' 'in righteousness He doth judge and make war.' And 'the armies which were in heaven' (Revelation 19:11, 14) follow Him. With anthems of celestial melody the holy angels, a vast, unnumbered throng, attend Him on His way. The firmament seems filled with radiant forms—'ten thousand times ten thousand, and thousands of thousands [Revelation 5:11].' No human pen can portray the scene; no mortal mind is adequate to conceive its splendor. 'His glory covered the heavens, and the earth was full of His praise. And

His brightness was as the light.' Habakkuk 3:3, 4. As the living cloud comes still nearer, every eye beholds the Prince of life. No crown of thorns now mars that sacred head; but a diadem of glory rests on His holy brow. His countenance outshines the dazzling brightness of the noonday sun. 'And He hath on His vesture and on His thigh a name written, *King of kings, and Lord of lords.*' Revelation 19:16."

1 Corinthians 15:52

"In a moment, in the twinkling of an eye, at the last trumpet. For the trumpet will sound, and the dead will be raised incorruptible, and we shall be changed."

Matthew 24:31

"And He will send His angels with a great sound of a trumpet, and they will gather together His elect from the four winds, from one end of heaven to the other."

The Great Controversy, p. 645

"The living righteous are changed 'in a moment, in the twinkling of an eye [1 Corinthians 15:52].' At the voice of God they were glorified; now they are made immortal and with the risen saints are caught up to meet their Lord in the air. Angels 'gather together His elect from the four winds, from one end of heaven to the other [Matthew 24:31].' Little children are borne by holy angels to their mothers' arms. Friends long separated by death are united, nevermore to part, and with songs of gladness ascend together to the City of God.

"On each side of the cloudy chariot are wings, and beneath it are living wheels; and as the chariot rolls upward, the wheels cry, 'Holy,' and the wings, as they move, cry, 'Holy,' and the retinue of angels cry, 'Holy, holy, holy, Lord God Almighty.' And the redeemed shout, 'Alleluia!' as the chariot moves onward toward the New Jerusalem."

The Great Controversy, p. 657

"At the coming of Christ the wicked are blotted from the face of the whole earth—consumed with the spirit of His mouth and destroyed by the brightness of His glory. Christ takes His people to the City of God, and the earth is emptied of its inhabitants."

Revelation 20:1–3

"Then I saw an angel coming down from heaven, having the key to the bottomless pit and a great chain in his hand. He laid hold of the dragon, that serpent of old, who is *the* Devil and Satan, and bound him for a thousand years; and he cast him into the bottomless pit, and shut him up, and set a seal on him, so that he should deceive the nations no more till the thousand years were finished. But after these things he must be released for a little while."

Leviticus 16:21

"Aaron shall lay both his hands on the head of the live goat, confess over it all the iniquities of the children of Israel, and all their transgressions, concerning all their sins, putting them on the head of the goat, and shall send *it* away into the wilderness by the hand of a suitable man."

The Great Controversy, pp. 657, 658

"The whole earth appears like a desolate wilderness. The ruins of cities and villages destroyed by the earthquake, uprooted trees, ragged rocks thrown out by the sea or torn out of the earth itself, are scattered over its surface, while vast caverns mark the spot where the mountains have been rent from their foundations.

"Now the event takes place foreshadowed in the last solemn service of the Day of Atonement. When the ministration in the holy of holies had been completed, and the sins of Israel had been removed from the sanctuary by virtue of the blood of the sin offering, then the scapegoat was presented alive before the Lord; and in the presence of the congregation the high priest confessed over him 'all the iniquities of the children of Israel, and all their transgressions in all their sins, putting them upon the head of the goat.' Leviticus 16:21. In like manner, when the work of atonement in the heavenly sanctuary has been completed, then in the presence of God and heavenly angels and the hosts of the redeemed the sins of God's people will be placed upon Satan; he will be declared guilty of all the evil which he has caused them to commit. And as the scapegoat was sent away into a land not inhabited, so Satan will be banished to the desolate earth, an uninhabited and dreary wilderness.

"The revelator foretells the banishment of Satan and the condition of chaos and desolation to which the earth is to be reduced, and he declares that this condition will exist for a thousand years. After presenting the scenes of the Lord's second coming and the destruction of the wicked, the prophecy continues: 'I saw an angel come down from heaven, having the key of the bottomless pit and a great chain in his hand. And he laid hold on the dragon, that old serpent, which is the devil, and Satan, and bound him a thousand years, and cast him into the bottomless pit, and shut him up, and set a seal upon him, that he should deceive the nations no more, till the thousand years should be fulfilled: and after that he must be loosed a little season.' Revelation 20:1–3."

The Judgment / The Sentencing Phase

Revelation 20:4–6
"And I saw thrones, and they sat on them, and judgment was committed to them. Then *I saw* the souls of those who had been beheaded for their witness to Jesus and for the word of God, who had not worshiped the beast or his image, and had not received *his* mark on their foreheads or on their hands. And they lived and reigned with Christ for a thousand years.... This *is* the first resurrection. Blessed and holy *is* he who has part in the first resurrection. Over such the second death has no power, but they shall be priests of God and of Christ, and shall reign with Him a thousand years."

The Judgment / The Execution Phase

Malachi 4:1, 2
" 'For behold, the day is coming, burning like an oven, and all the proud, yes, all who do wickedly will be stubble. And the day which is coming shall burn them up,' says the Lord of hosts, 'That will leave them neither root nor branch. But to you who fear My name the Sun of Righteousness shall arise with healing in His wings; and you shall go out and grow fat like stall-fed calves.' "

2 Peter 3:10
"But the day of the Lord will come as a thief in the night, in which the heavens will pass away with a great noise, and the elements will melt with fervent heat; both the earth and the works that are in it will be burned up."

Isaiah 34:8
"For *it is* the day of the Lord's vengeance, the year of recompense for the cause of Zion."

Psalm 28:4

"Give them according to their deeds, and according to the wickedness of their endeavors; give them according to the work of their hands; render to them what they deserve."

Isaiah 14:7

"The whole earth is at rest *and* quiet; they break forth into singing."

Revelation 19:6

"And I heard, as it were, the voice of a great multitude, as the sound of many waters and as the sound of mighty thunderings, saying, 'Alleluia! For the Lord God Omnipotent reigns!' "

Psalm 84:11

"For the Lord God *is* a sun and shield; the Lord will give grace and glory; no good *thing* will He withhold from those who walk uprightly."

The Great Controversy, **pp. 672, 673**

"Fire comes down from God out of heaven. The earth is broken up. The weapons concealed in its depths are drawn forth. Devouring flames burst from every yawning chasm. The very rocks are on fire. The day has come that shall burn as an oven. The elements melt with fervent heat, the earth also, and the works that are therein are burned up. Malachi 4:1; 2 Peter 3:10. The earth's surface seems one molten mass—a vast, seething lake of fire. It is the time of the judgment and perdition of ungodly men—'the day of the Lord's vengeance, and the year of recompenses for the controversy of Zion.' Isaiah 34:8.

"The wicked receive their recompense in the earth. Proverbs 11:31. They 'shall be stubble: and the day that cometh shall burn them up, saith the Lord of hosts.' Malachi 4:1. Some are destroyed as in a moment, while others

suffer many days. All are punished 'according to their deeds [Psalm 28:4].' The sins of the righteous having been transferred to Satan, he is made to suffer not only for his own rebellion, but for all the sins which he has caused God's people to commit. His punishment is to be far greater than that of those whom he has deceived. After all have perished who fell by his deceptions, he is still to live and suffer on. In the cleansing flames the wicked are at last destroyed, root and branch—Satan the root, his followers the branches. The full penalty of the law has been visited; the demands of justice have been met; and heaven and earth, beholding, declare the righteousness of Jehovah.

"Satan's work of ruin is forever ended. For six thousand years he has wrought his will, filling the earth with woe and causing grief throughout the universe. The whole creation has groaned and travailed together in pain. Now God's creatures are forever delivered from his presence and temptations. 'The whole earth is at rest, and is quiet: they [the righteous] break forth into singing.' Isaiah 14:7. And a shout of praise and triumph ascends from the whole loyal universe. 'The voice of a great multitude,' 'as the voice of many waters, and as the voice of mighty thunderings,' is heard, saying: 'Alleluia: for the Lord God omnipotent reigneth.' Revelation 19:6.

"While the earth was wrapped in the fire of destruction, the righteous abode safely in the Holy City. Upon those that had part in the first resurrection, the second death has no power. While God is to the wicked a consuming fire, He is to His people both a sun and a shield. Revelation 20:6; Psalm 84:11."

Restoration of the Kingdom of Glory

Revelation 21:1

"Now I saw a new heaven and a new earth, for the first heaven and the first earth had passed away. Also there was no more sea."

Isaiah 63:1

"Who *is* this who comes from Edom, with dyed garments from Bozrah, this *One who is* glorious in His apparel, traveling in the greatness of His strength?—'I who speak in righteousness, mighty to save.' "

Ephesians 1:14

"Who is the guarantee of our inheritance until the redemption of the purchased possession, to the praise of His glory."

Isaiah 45:18

"For thus says the Lord, Who created the heavens, Who is God, Who formed the earth and made it, Who has established it, Who did not create it in vain, Who formed it to be inhabited: 'I *am* the Lord, and *there is* no other.' "

Psalm 37:29

"The righteous shall inherit the land, and dwell in it forever."

The Great Controversy, p. 674

" 'I saw a new heaven and a new earth: for the first heaven and the first earth were passed away.' Revelation 21:1. The fire that consumes the wicked purifies the earth. Every trace of the curse is swept away. No eternally burning hell will keep before the ransomed the fearful consequences of sin.

"One reminder alone remains: Our Redeemer will ever bear the marks of His crucifixion. Upon His wounded head, upon His side, His hands and feet, are the only traces of the cruel work that sin has wrought. Says the prophet, beholding Christ in His glory: 'He had bright beams coming out of His side: and there was the hiding of His power.' Habakkuk 3:4, margin. That pierced side whence flowed the crimson stream that reconciled man to God—there is the Saviour's glory, there 'the hiding of His power.' 'Mighty to save [Isaiah 63:1],' through the sacrifice of redemption, He was therefore strong to execute justice upon them that despised God's mercy. And the tokens of His humiliation are His highest honor; through the eternal ages the wounds of Calvary will show forth His praise and declare His power.

" 'O Tower of the flock, the stronghold of the daughter of Zion, unto Thee shall it come, even the first dominion.' Micah 4:8. The time has come to which holy men have looked with longing since the flaming sword barred the first pair from Eden, the time for 'the redemption of the purchased possession.' Ephesians 1:14. The earth originally given to man as his kingdom, betrayed by him into the hands of Satan, and so long held by the mighty foe, has been brought back by the great plan of redemption. All that was lost by sin has been restored. 'Thus saith the Lord … that formed the earth and made it; He hath established it, He created it not in vain, He formed it to be inhabited.' Isaiah 45:18. God's original purpose in the creation of the earth is fulfilled as it is made the eternal abode of the redeemed. 'The righteous shall inherit the land, and dwell therein forever.' Psalm 37:29."

Isaiah 66:22, 23

" 'For as the new heavens and the new earth which I will make shall remain before Me,' says the Lord, 'So shall your descendants and your name remain. And it shall come to pass *that* from one New Moon to another, and from one Sabbath to another, all flesh shall come to worship before Me,' says the Lord."

The Great Controversy, **p. 678**

"The great controversy is ended. Sin and sinners are no more. The entire universe is clean. One pulse of harmony and gladness beats through the vast creation. From Him who created all, flow life and light and gladness, throughout the realms of illimitable space. From the minutest atom to the greatest world, all things, animate and inanimate, in their unshadowed beauty and perfect joy, declare that God is love."

"Here is the patience of the saints; here are those who
keep the commandments of God and the faith of Jesus."
Revelation 14:12

"I was shown three steps—the first, second, and third angels' messages."

"These messages were represented to me as an anchor to the
people of God. Those who understand and receive them will be
kept from being swept away by the many delusions of Satan."
Early Writings, pp. 258, 256

Chapter 9

The Three Angels' Messages

Introduction

Revelation 14:6–12

"Then I saw another angel flying in the midst of heaven, having the everlasting gospel to preach to those who dwell on the earth—to every nation, tribe, tongue, and people—saying with a loud voice, 'Fear God and give glory to Him, for the hour of His judgment has come; and worship Him who made heaven and earth, the sea and springs of water.'

"And another angel followed, saying, 'Babylon is fallen, is fallen, that great city, because she has made all nations drink of the wine of the wrath of her fornication.'

"Then a third angel followed them, saying with a loud voice, 'If anyone worships the beast and his image, and receives *his* mark on his forehead or on his hand, he himself shall also drink of the wine of the wrath of God, which is poured out full strength into the cup of His indignation. He shall be tormented with fire and brimstone in the presence of the holy angels and in the presence of the Lamb. And the smoke of their torment ascends forever and ever; and they have no rest day or night, who worship the beast and his image, and whoever receives the mark of his name.'

"Here is the patience of the saints; here *are* those who keep the commandments of God and the faith of Jesus."

Revelation 14:15

"And another angel came out of the temple, crying with a loud voice to Him who sat on the cloud, 'Thrust in Your sickle and reap, for the time has come for You to reap, for the harvest of the earth is ripe.' "

***The Great Controversy*, p. 311**

"To prepare a people to stand in the day of God, a great work of reform was to be accomplished. God saw that many of His professed people were not building for eternity, and in His mercy He was about to send a message of warning to arouse them from their stupor and lead them to make ready for the coming of the Lord.

"This warning is brought to view in Revelation 14 [verses 6–12]. Here is a threefold message represented as proclaimed by heavenly beings and immediately followed by the coming of the Son of man to reap 'the harvest of the earth [Revelation 14:15].' The first of these warnings announces the approaching judgment. The prophet beheld an angel flying 'in the midst of heaven, having the everlasting gospel to preach unto them that dwell on the earth, and to every nation, and kindred, and tongue, and people, saying with a loud voice, Fear God, and give glory to Him; for the hour of His judgment is come: and worship Him that made heaven, and earth, and the sea, and the fountains of waters.' Revelation 14:6, 7."

Ecclesiastes 12:13

"Let us hear the conclusion of the whole matter: Fear God and keep His commandments, for this is man's all."

1 John 5:3

"For this is the love of God, that we keep His commandments. And His commandments are not burdensome."

Proverbs 28:9

"One who turns away his ear from hearing the law, even his prayer *is* an abomination."

The Great Controversy, **p. 436**

"By the first angel, men are called upon to 'fear God, and give glory to Him [Revelation 14:7]' and to worship Him as the Creator of the heavens and the earth. In order to do this, they must obey His law. Says the wise man: 'Fear God, and keep His commandments: for this is the whole duty of man.' Ecclesiastes 12:13. Without obedience to His commandments no worship can be pleasing to God. 'This is the love of God, that we keep His commandments.' 'He that turneth away his ear from hearing the law, even his prayer shall be abomination.' 1 John 5:3; Proverbs 28:9."

The Great Controversy, **pp. 435, 436**

"Those who had accepted the light concerning the mediation of Christ and the perpetuity of the law of God found that these were the truths presented in Revelation 14. The messages of this chapter constitute a threefold warning which is to prepare the inhabitants of the earth for the Lord's second coming. The announcement, 'The hour of His judgment is come [Revelation 14:7],' points to the closing work of Christ's ministration for the salvation of men. It heralds a truth which must be proclaimed until the Saviour's intercession shall cease and He shall return to the earth to take His people to Himself. The work of judgment which began in 1844 must continue until the cases of all are decided, both of the living and

the dead; hence it will extend to the close of human probation."

Ezekiel 33:7

"So you, son of man: I have made you a watchman for the house of Israel; therefore you shall hear a word from My mouth and warn them for Me."

The Great Controversy, **p. 380**

"But the churches generally did not accept the warning. Their ministers, who, as watchmen 'unto the house of Israel [Ezekiel 33:7],' should have been the first to discern the tokens of Jesus' coming, had failed to learn the truth either from the testimony of the prophets or from the the signs of the times."

The Great Controversy, **pp. 380, 381**

"In refusing the warning of the first angel, they rejected the means which Heaven had provided for their restoration. They spurned the gracious messenger that would have corrected the evils which separated them from God, and with greater eagerness they turned to seek the friendship of the world. Here was the cause of that fearful condition of worldliness, backsliding, and spiritual death which existed in the churches in 1844.

"In Revelation 14 the first angel is followed by a second proclaiming: 'Babylon is fallen, is fallen, that great city, because she made all nations drink of the wine of the wrath of her fornication.' Revelation 14:8. The term 'Babylon' is derived from 'Babel,' and signifies confusion. It is employed in Scripture to designate the various forms of false or apostate religion. In Revelation 17 Babylon is represented as a woman—a figure which is used in the Bible as the symbol of a church, a virtuous woman representing a pure church, a vile woman an apostate church."

Exodus 20:10, 11

"But the seventh day *is* the Sabbath of the Lord your God. *In it* you shall do no work: you, nor your son, nor your daughter, nor your male servant, nor your female servant, nor your cattle, nor your stranger who *is* within your gates. For *in* six days the Lord made the heavens and the earth, the sea, and all that *is* in them, and rested the seventh day. Therefore the Lord blessed the Sabbath day and hallowed it."

The Great Controversy, p. 437

"In Revelation 14, men are called upon to worship the Creator; and the prophecy brings to view a class that, as the result of the threefold message, are keeping the commandments of God. One of these commandments points directly to God as the Creator. The fourth precept declares: 'The seventh day is the Sabbath of the Lord thy God: … for in six days the Lord made heaven and earth, the sea, and all that in them is, and rested the seventh day: wherefore the Lord blessed the Sabbath day, and hallowed it.' Exodus 20:10, 11."

The Great Controversy, p. 438

"In contrast to those who keep the commandments of God and have the faith of Jesus, the third angel points to another class, against whose errors a solemn and fearful warning is uttered: 'If any man worship the beast and his image, and receive his mark in his forehead, or in his hand, the same shall drink of the wine of the wrath of God.' Revelation 14:9, 10. A correct interpretation of the symbols employed is necessary to an understanding of this message. What is represented by the beast, the image, the mark?"

The Great Controversy, pp. 449, 450

"The most fearful threatening ever addressed to mortals is contained in the third angel's message. That must be a terrible sin which calls down the wrath of God unmingled with mercy. Men are not to be left in darkness concerning this important matter; the warning against this sin is to be given to the world before the visitation of God's judgments, that all may know why they are to be inflicted, and have opportunity to escape them. Prophecy declares that the first angel would make his announcement to 'every nation, and kindred, and tongue, and people [Revelation 14:6].' The warning of the third angel, which forms a part of the same threefold message, is to be no less widespread. It is represented in the prophecy as being proclaimed with a loud voice, by an angel flying in the midst of heaven; and it will command the attention of the world."

The First Angel's Message / The Gospel (Revelation 14:6)

Revelation 14:6

"Then I saw another angel flying in the midst of heaven, having the everlasting gospel to preach to those who dwell on the earth—to every nation, tribe, tongue, and people—"

Two Definitions of the New Covenant (the Everlasting Gospel)

Patriarchs and Prophets, p. 371

"This covenant … was simply an arrangement for bringing men again into harmony with the divine will, placing them where they could obey God's law."

Education, p. 125

"The redemption plan [is] the restoration in the human soul of the image of God."

A few of many other names or phrases that refer to the gospel	
Covenant of Grace	PP 370*
My Covenant	Genesis 17:7; PP 370
Everlasting Covenant	Psalm 111:9; Genesis 17:7
New Covenant	Jeremiah 31:31; Hebrews 8:8, 13; 12:24; PP 371
Abrahamic Covenant	PP 370, 371
Second Covenant	GC 413**; PP 371
Plan of Redemption	Psalm 111:9; Hebrews 9:12; PP 64
Plan of Salvation	PP 63
Covenant of Peace	Ezekiel 37:26
Unsearchable Riches of Christ	Ephesians 3:8
Mystery of God	Ephesians 3:9; Colossians 2:2; Revelation 10:7
Wisdom of God	Ephesians 3:10
His Eternal Purpose	Ephesians 3:11
Eternal Redemption	Hebrews 9:12
Everlasting or Eternal Gospel	Revelation 14:6

* PP - *Patriarchs and Prophets*   ** GC - *The Great Controversy*

Romans 1:1, 2, 16, 17

"Paul, a bondservant of Jesus Christ, called *to be* an apostle, separated to the gospel of God which He promised before through His prophets in the Holy Scriptures."

"For I am not ashamed of the gospel of Christ, for it is the power of God to salvation for everyone who believes, for the Jew first and also for the Greek. For in it the righteousness of God is revealed from faith to faith; as it is written, 'The just shall live by faith.' "

1 Corinthians 15:1–4

"Moreover, brethren, I declare to you the gospel which I preached to you, which also you received and in which you stand, by which also you are saved, if you hold fast that word which I preached to you—unless you believed in vain.

"For I delivered to you first of all that which I also received: that Christ died for our sins according to the Scriptures, and that He was buried, and that He rose again the third day according to the Scriptures."

Matthew 24:14

"And this gospel of the kingdom will be preached in all the world as a witness to all the nations, and then the end will come."

Mark 13:10

"And the gospel must first be preached to all the nations."

***The Great Controversy*, p. 355**

"A Great religious awakening under the proclamation of Christ's soon coming is foretold in the prophecy of the first angel's message of Revelation 14. An angel is seen flying 'in the midst of heaven, having the everlasting gospel to preach unto them that dwell on the earth, and to every nation, and kindred, and tongue, and people.' 'With a loud voice' he proclaims the message: 'Fear God, and give glory to Him; for the hour of His judgment is come: and worship Him that made heaven, and earth, and the sea, and the fountains of waters.' Verses 6, 7."

The Great Controversy, p. 312
"This message [Revelation 14:6, 7] is declared to be a part of 'the everlasting gospel.' The work of preaching the gospel has not been committed to angels, but has been entrusted to men. Holy angels have been employed in directing this work, they have in charge the great movements for the salvation of men; but the actual proclamation of the gospel is performed by the servants of Christ upon the earth."

The First Angel's Message / The Judgment (Revelation 14:7)

Revelation 14:7
"Saying with a loud voice, 'Fear God and give glory to Him, for the hour of His judgment has come; and worship Him who made heaven and earth, the sea and springs of water.' "

Revelation 22:12
"And behold, I am coming quickly, and My reward *is* with Me, to give to every one according to his work."

The Great Controversy, p. 352
"In the typical system, which was a shadow of the sacrifice and priesthood of Christ, the cleansing of the sanctuary was the last service performed by the high priest in the yearly round of ministration. It was the closing work of the atonement—a removal or putting away of sin from Israel. It prefigured the closing work in the ministration of our High Priest in heaven, in the removal or blotting out of the sins of His people, which are registered in the heavenly records. This service involves a work of investigation, a work of judgment; and it immediately precedes the coming of Christ in the clouds of heaven with power and great glory; for when He comes, every case has been decided. Says Jesus: 'My reward is with Me, to give every man according as his work shall be.' Revelation 22:12. It is this work of judgment, immediately preceding the second advent, that is announced in the first angel's message of Revelation 14:7: 'Fear God, and give glory to Him; for the hour of His judgment is come.' "

The Great Controversy, pp. 355, 356
"The message itself sheds light as to the time when this movement is to take place. It is declared to be a part of the 'everlasting gospel;' and it announces the opening of the judgment. The message of salvation has been preached in all ages; but this message is a part of the gospel which could be proclaimed only in the last days, for only then would it be true that the hour of judgment *had come*."

Daniel 8:14
"And he said to me, 'For two thousand three hundred days; then the sanctuary shall be cleansed.' "

The Great Controversy, p. 424
"Both the prophecy of Daniel 8:14, 'Unto two thousand and three hundred days; then shall the sanctuary be cleansed,' and the first angel's message, 'Fear God, and give glory to Him; for the hour of His judgment is come,'

pointed to Christ's ministration in the most holy place, to the investigative judgment, and not to the coming of Christ for the redemption of His people and the destruction of the wicked."

The Investigative Phase of the Judgment

Revelation 10:7
"But in the days of the sounding of the seventh angel, when he is about to sound, the mystery of God would be finished, as He declared to His servants the prophets."

Revelation 11:15–19
"Then the seventh angel sounded: And there were loud voices in heaven, saying, 'The kingdoms of this world have become *the kingdoms* of our Lord and of His Christ, and He shall reign forever and ever!' And the twenty-four elders who sat before God on their thrones fell on their faces and worshiped God, saying: 'We give You thanks, O Lord God Almighty, The One who is and who was and who is to come, because You have taken Your great power and reigned. The nations were angry, and Your wrath has come, and the time of the dead, that they should be judged, and that You should reward Your servants the prophets and the saints, and those who fear Your name, small and great, and should destroy those who destroy the earth.'

"Then the temple of God was opened in heaven, and the ark of His covenant was seen in His temple. And there were lightnings, noises, thunderings, an earthquake, and great hail."

Daniel 7:9, 10, 13
"I watched till thrones were put in place, and the Ancient of Days was seated; His garment *was* white as snow, and the hair of His head

was like pure wool. His throne *was* a fiery flame, its wheels a burning fire; a fiery stream issued and came forth from before Him. A thousand thousands ministered to Him; ten thousand times ten thousand stood before Him. The court was seated, and the books were opened."

"I was watching in the night visions, and behold, *One* like the Son of Man, coming with the clouds of heaven! He came to the Ancient of Days, and they brought Him near before Him."

Revelation 20:12, 13
"And I saw the dead, small and great, standing before God, and books were opened. And another book was opened, which is *the Book* of Life. And the dead were judged according to their works, by the things which were written in the books. The sea gave up the dead who were in it, and Death and Hades delivered up the dead who were in them. And they were judged, each one according to his works."

Psalm 90:2
"Before the mountains were brought forth, or ever You had formed the earth and the world, even from everlasting to everlasting, You *are* God."

Malachi 3:1–3
" 'Behold, I send My messenger, and he will prepare the way before Me. And the Lord, whom you seek, will suddenly come to His temple, even the Messenger of the covenant, in whom you delight. Behold, He is coming,' says the Lord of hosts.

"But who can endure the day of His coming? And who can stand when He appears? For He *is* like a refiner's fire and like launderers' soap. He will sit as a refiner and a purifier of silver; He will purify the sons of Levi, and purge them as gold and silver, that they may offer to the Lord an offering in righteousness."

The Great Controversy, p. 479

" 'I beheld,' says the prophet Daniel, 'till thrones were placed, and One that was Ancient of Days did sit: His raiment was white as snow, and the hair of His head like pure wool; His throne was fiery flames, and the wheels thereof burning fire. A fiery stream issued and came forth from before Him: thousand thousands ministered unto Him, and ten thousand times ten thousand stood before Him: the judgment was set, and the books were opened.' Daniel 7:9, 10, R.V.

"Thus was presented to the prophet's vision the great and solemn day when the characters and the lives of men should pass in review before the Judge of all the earth, and to every man should be rendered 'according to his works [Revelation 20:13].' The Ancient of Days is God the Father. Says the psalmist: 'Before the mountains were brought forth, or ever Thou hadst formed the earth and the world, even from everlasting to everlasting, Thou art God.' Psalm 90:2. It is He, the source of all being, and the fountain of all law, that is to preside in the judgment. And holy angels as ministers and witnesses, in number 'ten thousand times ten thousand, and thousands of thousands,' attend this great tribunal."

The Great Controversy, p. 400

"The tenth day of the seventh month, the great Day of Atonement, the time of the cleansing of the sanctuary, which in the year 1844 fell upon the twenty-second of October, was regarded as the time of the Lord's coming."

Matthew 22:1–14

"And Jesus answered and spoke to them again by parables and said: 'The kingdom of heaven is like a certain king who arranged a marriage for his son, and sent out his servants to call those who were invited to the wedding; and they were not willing to come. Again, he sent out other servants, saying, "Tell those who are invited, 'See, I have prepared my dinner; my oxen and fatted cattle *are* killed, and all things *are* ready. Come to the wedding.' " But they made light of it and went their ways, one to his own farm, another to his business. And the rest seized his servants, treated *them* spitefully, and killed *them*. But when the king heard *about it*, he was furious. And he sent out his armies, destroyed those murderers, and burned up their city. Then he said to his servants, "The wedding is ready, but those who were invited were not worthy. Therefore go into the highways, and as many as you find, invite to the wedding." So those servants went out into the highways and gathered together all whom they found, both bad and good. And the wedding *hall* was filled with guests.

" 'But when the king came in to see the guests, he saw a man there who did not have on a wedding garment. So he said to him, "Friend, how did you come in here without a wedding garment?" And he was speechless. Then the king said to the servants, "Bind him hand and foot, take him away, and cast *him* into outer darkness; there will be weeping and gnashing of teeth."

" 'For many are called, but few *are* chosen.' "

Matthew 25:1–12

"Then the kingdom of heaven shall be likened to ten virgins who took their lamps and went out to meet the bridegroom. Now five of them were wise, and five *were* foolish. Those who *were* foolish took their lamps and took no oil with them, but the wise took oil in their vessels with their lamps. But while the bridegroom was delayed, they all slumbered and slept.

"And at midnight a cry was *heard*: 'Behold, the bridegroom is coming; go out to meet him!' Then all those virgins arose and trimmed their lamps. And the foolish said to the wise, 'Give us *some* of your oil, for our lamps are going out.' But the wise answered, saying, '*No*, lest there should not be enough for us and you; but go rather to those who sell, and buy for yourselves.' And while they went to buy, the bridegroom came, and those who were ready went in with him to the wedding; and the door was shut.

"Afterward the other virgins came also, saying, 'Lord, Lord, open to us!' But he answered and said, 'Assuredly, I say to you, I do not know you.' "

Revelation 21:9, 10
"Then one of the seven angels who had the seven bowls filled with the seven last plagues came to me and talked with me, saying, 'Come, I will show you the bride, the Lamb's wife.' And he carried me away in the Spirit to a great and high mountain, and showed me the great city, the holy Jerusalem, descending out of heaven from God."

Revelation 19:9
"Then he said to me, 'Write: "Blessed *are* those who are called to the marriage supper of the Lamb!" ' And he said to me, 'These are the true sayings of God.' "

Daniel 7:14
"Then to Him was given dominion and glory and a kingdom, that all peoples, nations, and languages should serve Him. His dominion *is* an everlasting dominion, which shall not pass away, and His kingdom *the one* which shall not be destroyed."

Revelation 21:2
"Then I, John, saw the holy city, New Jerusalem, coming down out of heaven from God, prepared as a bride adorned for her husband."

Matthew 8:11
"And I say to you that many will come from east and west, and sit down with Abraham, Isaac, and Jacob in the kingdom of heaven."

Luke 22:30
"That you may eat and drink at My table in My kingdom, and sit on thrones judging the twelve tribes of Israel."

Luke 12:36
"And you yourselves be like men who wait for their master, when he will return from the wedding, that when he comes and knocks they may open to him immediately."

The Great Controversy, **pp. 426–428**
"The coming of Christ as our high priest to the most holy place, for the cleansing of the sanctuary, brought to view in Daniel 8:14; the coming of the Son of man to the Ancient of Days, as presented in Daniel 7:13; and the coming of the Lord to His temple, foretold by Malachi, are descriptions of the same event; and this is also represented by the coming of the bridegroom to the marriage, described by Christ in the parable of the ten virgins, of Matthew 25.

"In the summer and autumn of 1844 the proclamation, 'Behold, the Bridegroom cometh,' was given. The two classes represented by the wise and foolish virgins were then developed—one class who looked with joy to the Lord's appearing, and who had been diligently preparing to meet Him; another class that, influenced by fear and acting from impulse, had been satisfied with a theory of the truth, but were destitute of the grace of God. In the parable, when the bridegroom came, 'they that were ready went in with him to the marriage.' The coming of the bridegroom, here brought to view, takes place before the marriage. The marriage represents the reception by Christ of His kingdom. The Holy City, the New Jerusalem, which is the capital and representative of the kingdom, is called 'the bride, the Lamb's wife.' Said the angel to John: 'Come hither, I will show thee the bride, the Lamb's wife.' 'He carried me away in the spirit,' says the prophet, 'and showed me that great city, the holy Jerusalem, descending out of heaven from God.' Revelation 21:9, 10. Clearly, then, the bride represents the Holy City, and the virgins that go out to meet the bridegroom are a symbol of the church. In the Revelation the people of God are said to be the guests at the marriage supper. Revelation 19:9. If *guests*, they cannot be represented also as the *bride*. Christ, as stated by the prophet Daniel, will receive from the Ancient of Days in heaven, 'dominion, and glory, and a kingdom;' He will receive the New Jerusalem, the capital of His kingdom, 'prepared as a bride adorned for her husband.' Daniel 7:14; Revelation 21:2. Having received the kingdom, He will come in His glory, as King of kings and Lord of lords, for the redemption of His people, who are to 'sit down with Abraham, and Isaac, and Jacob,' at His table in His kingdom (Matthew 8:11; Luke 22:30), to partake of the marriage supper of the Lamb.

"The proclamation, 'Behold, the Bridegroom cometh,' in the summer of 1844, led thousands to expect the immediate advent of the Lord. At the appointed time the Bridegroom came, not to the earth, as the people expected, but to the Ancient of Days in heaven, to the marriage, the reception of His kingdom. 'They that were ready went in

with Him to the marriage: and the door was shut.' They were not to be present in person at the marriage; for it takes place in heaven, while they are upon the earth. The followers of Christ are to 'wait for their Lord, when He will *return from* the wedding.' Luke 12:36. But they are to understand His work, and to follow Him by faith as He goes in before God. It is in this sense that they are said to go in to the marriage.

"In the parable it was those that had oil in their vessels with their lamps that went in to the marriage. Those who, with a knowledge of the truth from the Scriptures, had also the Spirit and grace of God, and who, in the night of their bitter trial, had patiently waited, searching the Bible for clearer light—these saw the truth concerning the sanctuary in heaven and the Saviour's change in ministration, and by faith they followed Him in His work in the sanctuary above. And all who through the testimony of the Scriptures accept the same truths, following Christ by faith as He enters in before God to perform the last work of mediation, and at its close to receive His kingdom—all these are represented as going in to the marriage.

"In the parable of Matthew 22 the same figure of the marriage is introduced, and the investigative judgment is clearly represented as taking place before the marriage. Previous to the wedding the king comes in to see the guests, to see if all are attired in the wedding garment, the spotless robe of character washed and made white in the blood of the Lamb. Matthew 22:11; Revelation 7:14. He who is found wanting is cast out, but all who upon examination are seen to have the wedding garment on are accepted of God and accounted worthy of a share in His kingdom and a seat upon His throne. This work of examination of character, of determining who are prepared for the kingdom of God, is that of the investigative judgment, the closing of work in the sanctuary above.

"When the work of investigation shall be ended, when the cases of those who in all ages have professed to be followers of Christ have been examined and decided, then, and not till then, probation will close, and the door of mercy will be shut. Thus in the one short sentence, 'They that were ready went in with Him to the marriage: and the door was shut,' we are carried down through the Saviour's final ministration, to the time when the great work for man's salvation shall be completed."

Hebrews 9:24–28

"For Christ has not entered the holy places made with hands, *which are* copies of the true, but into heaven itself, now to appear in the presence of God for us; not that He should offer Himself often, as the high priest enters the Most Holy Place every year with blood of another—He then would have had to suffer often since the foundation of the world; but now, once at the end of the ages, He has appeared to put away sin by the sacrifice of Himself. And as it is appointed for men to die once, but after this the judgment, so Christ was offered once to bear the sins of many. To those who eagerly wait for Him He will appear a second time, apart from sin, for salvation."

The Sentencing Phase of the Judgment

1 Corinthians 4:5

"Therefore judge nothing before the time, until the Lord comes, who will both bring to light the hidden things of darkness and reveal the counsels of the hearts. Then each one's praise will come from God."

Daniel 7:22

"Until the Ancient of Days came, and a judgment was made *in favor* of the saints of the Most High, and the time came for the saints to possess the kingdom."

Revelation 20:4–6

"And I saw thrones, and they sat on them, and judgment was committed to them. Then *I saw* the souls of those who had been beheaded for their witness to Jesus and for the word of God, who had not worshiped the beast or his image, and had not received *his* mark on their foreheads or on their hands. And they lived and reigned with Christ for a thousand years.... Blessed and holy *is* he who has part in the first resurrection. Over such the second death has no power, but they shall be priests of God and of Christ, and shall reign with Him a thousand years."

1 Corinthians 6:2, 3

"Do you not know that the saints will judge the world? And if the world will be judged by you, are you unworthy to judge the smallest matters? Do you not know that we shall judge angels? How much more, things that pertain to this life?"

Jude 6

"And the angels who did not keep their proper domain, but left their own abode, He has reserved in everlasting chains under darkness for the judgment of the great day."

The Great Controversy, pp. 660, 661

"During the thousand years between the first and the second resurrection the judgment of the wicked takes place. The apostle Paul points to this judgment as an event that follows the second advent. 'Judge nothing before the time, until the Lord come, who both will bring to light the hidden things of darkness, and will make manifest the counsels of the hearts.' 1 Corinthians 4:5. Daniel declares that when the Ancient of Days came, 'judgment was given to the saints of the Most High.' Daniel 7:22. At this time the righteous reign as kings and priests unto God. John in the Revelation says: 'I saw thrones, and they sat upon them, and judgment was given unto them.' 'They shall be priests of God and of Christ, and shall reign with Him a thousand years.' Revelation 20:4, 6. It is at this time that, as foretold by Paul, 'the saints shall judge the world.' 1 Corinthians 6:2. In union with Christ they judge the wicked, comparing their acts with the statute book, the Bible, and deciding every case according to the deeds done in the body. Then the portion which the wicked must suffer is meted out, according to their works; and it is recorded against their names in the book of death.

"Satan also and evil angels are judged by Christ and His people. Says Paul: 'Know ye not that we shall judge angels?' Verse 3. And Jude declares that 'the angels which kept not their first estate, but left their own habitation, He hath reserved in everlasting chains under darkness unto the judgment of the great day.' Jude 6."

The Execution Phase of the Judgment

Revelation 20:5
"But the rest of the dead did not live again until the thousand years were finished."

Isaiah 24:22
"They will be gathered together, *as* prisoners are gathered in the pit, and will be shut up in the prison; after many days they will be punished."

The Great Controversy, p. 661
"At the close of the thousand years the second resurrection will take place. Then the wicked will be raised from the dead and appear before God for the execution of 'the judgment written.' Thus the revelator, after describing the resurrection of the righteous, says: 'The rest of the dead lived not again until the thousand years were finished.' Revelation 20:5. And Isaiah declares, concerning the wicked: 'They shall be gathered together, as prisoners are gathered in the pit, and shall be shut up in the prison, and *after many days shall they be visited*.' Isaiah 24:22."

Revelation 20:7–9 (first part)
"Now when the thousand years have expired, Satan will be released from his prison and will go out to deceive the nations which are in the four corners of the earth, Gog and Magog, to gather them together to battle, whose number *is* as the sand of the sea. They went up on the breadth of the earth and surrounded the camp of the saints and the beloved city."

The Great Controversy, p. 662
"At the close of the thousand years, Christ again returns to the earth. He is accompanied by the host of the redeemed and attended by a retinue of angels. As He descends in terrific majesty He bids the wicked dead arise to receive their doom. They come forth, a mighty host, numberless as the sands of the sea. What a contrast to those who were raised at the first resurrection! The righteous were clothed with immortal youth and beauty. The wicked bear the traces of disease and death."

The Great Controversy, p. 663
"Now Satan prepares for a last mighty struggle for the supremacy.... He represents himself to his deluded subjects as a redeemer, assuring

them that his power has brought them forth from their graves and that he is about to rescue them from the most cruel tyranny. The presence of Christ having been removed, Satan works wonders to support his claims. He makes the weak strong and inspires all with his own spirit and energy. He proposes to lead them against the camp of the saints and to take possession of the City of God. With fiendish exultation he points to the unnumbered millions who have been raised from the dead and declares that as their leader he is well able to overthrow the city and regain his throne and his kingdom."

The Great Controversy, p. 664

"Satan, the mightiest of warriors, leads the van, and his angels unite their forces for this final struggle. Kings and warriors are in his train, and the multitudes follow in vast companies, each under its appointed leader. With military precision the serried ranks advance over the earth's broken and uneven surface to the City of God. By command of Jesus, the gates of the New Jerusalem are closed, and the armies of Satan surround the city and make ready for the onset."

Revelation 20:11–13

"Then I saw a great white throne and Him who sat on it, from whose face the earth and the heaven fled away. And there was found no place for them. And I saw the dead, small and great, standing before God, and books were opened. And another book was opened, which is *the Book* of Life. And the dead were judged according to their works, by the things which were written in the books. The sea gave up the dead who were in it, and Death and Hades delivered up the dead who were in them. And they were judged, each one according to his works."

The Great Controversy, p. 665

"Now Christ again appears to the view of His enemies. Far above the city, upon a foundation of burnished gold, is a throne, high and lifted up. Upon this throne sits the Son of God, and around Him are the subjects of His kingdom. The power and majesty of Christ no language can describe, no pen portray. The glory of the Eternal Father is enshrouding His Son. The brightness of His presence fills the City of God, and flows out beyond the gates, flooding the whole earth with its radiance."

The Great Controversy, p. 666

"In the presence of the assembled inhabitants of earth and heaven the final coronation of the Son of God takes place. And now, invested with supreme majesty and power, the King of kings pronounces sentence upon the rebels against His government and executes justice upon those who have transgressed His law and oppressed His people. Says the prophet of God: 'I saw a great white throne, and Him that sat on it, from whose face the earth and the heaven fled away; and there was found no place for them. And I saw the dead, small and great, stand before God; and the books were opened: and another book was opened, which is the book of life: and the dead were judged out of those things which were written in the books, according to their works.' Revelation 20:11, 12."

Revelation 20:9 (last part), 14, 15, 10

"And fire came down from God out of heaven and devoured them."

"Then Death and Hades were cast into the lake of fire. This is the second death. And anyone not found written in the Book of Life was cast into the lake of fire."

"The devil, who deceived them, was cast into the lake of fire and brimstone where the beast and the false prophet *are*. And they will be tormented day and night forever and ever."

Malachi 4:1

" 'For behold, the day is coming, burning like an oven, and all the proud, yes, all who do wickedly will be stubble. And the day which is coming shall burn them up,' says the Lord of hosts, 'That will leave them neither root nor branch.' "

2 Peter 3:10

"But the day of the Lord will come as a thief in the night, in which the heavens will pass away with a great noise, and the elements will melt with fervent heat; both the earth and the works that are in it will be burned up."

Isaiah 34:8

"For *it is* the day of the Lord's vengeance, the year of recompense for the cause of Zion."

The Great Controversy, pp. 672, 673

"Fire comes down from God out of heaven. The earth is broken up. The weapons concealed in its depths are drawn forth. Devouring flames burst from every yawning chasm. The very rocks are on fire. The day has come that shall burn as an oven. The elements melt with fervent heat, the earth also, and the works that are therein are burned up. Malachi 4:1; 2 Peter 3:10. The earth's surface seems one molten mass—a vast, seething lake of fire. It is the time of the judgment and perdition of ungodly men—'the day of the Lord's vengeance, and the year of recompenses for the controversy of Zion.' Isaiah 34:8."

The Second Angel's Message

Revelation 14:8

"And another angel followed, saying, 'Babylon is fallen, is fallen, that great city, because she has made all nations drink of the wine of the wrath of her fornication.' "

Ezekiel 16:13–15, 32

" 'Thus you were adorned with gold and silver, and your clothing *was of* fine linen, silk, and embroidered cloth. You ate *pastry of* fine flour, honey, and oil. You were exceedingly beautiful, and succeeded to royalty. Your fame went out among the nations because of your beauty, for it *was* perfect through My splendor which I had bestowed on you,' says the Lord God. 'But you trusted in your own beauty, played the harlot because of your fame, and poured out your harlotry on everyone passing by who *would have* it.' "

" '*You are* an adulterous wife, *who* takes strangers instead of her husband.' "

Jeremiah 3:20

" 'Surely, *as* a wife treacherously departs from her husband, so have you dealt treacherously with Me, O house of Israel,' says the Lord."

Jeremiah 51:7, 8

"Babylon *was* a golden cup in the Lord's hand, that made all the earth drunk. The nations drank her wine; therefore the nations are deranged. Babylon has suddenly fallen and been destroyed. Wail for her! Take balm for her pain; perhaps she may be healed."

Revelation 17:1–6, 18

"Then one of the seven angels who had the seven bowls came and talked with me, saying to me, 'Come, I will show you the judgment of the great harlot who sits on many waters, with whom the kings of the earth committed fornication, and the inhabitants of the earth were made drunk with the wine of her fornication.'

"So he carried me away in the Spirit into the wilderness. And I saw a woman sitting on a scarlet beast *which was* full of names of blasphemy, having seven heads and ten horns. The woman was arrayed in purple and scarlet, and adorned with gold and precious stones and pearls, having in her hand a golden cup full of abominations and the filthiness of her fornication. And on her forehead a name *was* written: MYSTERY, BABYLON THE GREAT, THE MOTHER OF HARLOTS AND OF THE ABOMINATIONS OF THE EARTH.

"I saw the woman, drunk with the blood of the saints and with the blood of the martyrs of Jesus. And when I saw her, I marveled with great amazement."

"And the woman whom you saw is that great city which reigns over the kings of the earth."

The Great Controversy, p. 381

"In Revelation 14 the first angel is followed by a second proclaiming: 'Babylon is fallen, is fallen, that great city, because she made all nations drink of the wine of the wrath of her fornication.' Revelation 14:8. The term 'Babylon' is derived from 'Babel,' and signifies confusion. It is employed in Scripture to designate the various forms of false or apostate religion. In Revelation 17 Babylon is represented as a woman—a figure which is used in the Bible as the symbol of a church, a virtuous woman representing a pure church, a vile woman an apostate church."

The Great Controversy, pp. 382, 383

"Babylon is said to be 'the *mother* of harlots [Revelation17:5].' By her *daughters* must be symbolized churches that cling to her doctrines and traditions, and follow her example of sacrificing the truth and the approval of God, in order to form an unlawful alliance with the world. The message of Revelation 14, announcing the *fall* of Babylon must apply to religious bodies that were once pure and have become corrupt."

The Great Controversy, p. 389

"The second angel's message of Revelation 14 was first preached in the summer of 1844, and it then had a more direct application to the churches of the United States, where the warning of the judgment had been most widely proclaimed and most generally rejected, and where the declension in the churches had been most rapid. But the message of the second angel did not reach its complete fulfillment in 1844. The churches then experienced a moral fall, in consequence of their refusal of the light of the advent message; but that fall was not complete."

1 Timothy 3:15

"But if I am delayed, I *write* so that you may know how you ought to conduct yourself in the house of God, which is the church of the living God, the pillar and ground of the truth."

The Great Controversy, p. 376

"As his [William Miller's] work tended to build up the churches, it was for a time regarded with favor. But as ministers and religious leaders decided against the advent doctrine and desired to suppress all agitation of the subject, they not only opposed it from the pulpit, but denied their members the privilege of attending preaching upon the second advent, or even of speaking of their hope in the social meetings of the church. Thus the believers found themselves in a position of great trial and perplexity. They loved their churches and were loath to separate from them; but as they saw the testimony of God's word suppressed and their right to investigate the prophecies denied they felt that loyalty to God forbade them to submit. Those who sought to shut out the testimony of God's word they could not regard as constituting the church of Christ, 'the pillar and ground of the truth [1 Timothy 3:15].' Hence they felt themselves justified in separating from their former connection. In the summer of 1844 about fifty thousand withdrew from the churches."

Isaiah 29:9, 10, 13

"Pause and wonder! Blind yourselves and be blind! They are drunk, but not with wine; they stagger, but not with intoxicating drink. For the Lord has poured out on you the spirit of deep sleep, and has closed your eyes, namely, the prophets; and He has covered your heads, *namely*, the seers."

"Inasmuch as these people draw near with their mouths and honor Me with their lips, but have removed their hearts far from Me, and their fear toward Me is taught by the commandment of men."

Micah 3:5–7

"Thus says the Lord concerning the prophets who make my people stray; who chant 'Peace' while they chew with their teeth, but who prepare war against him who puts nothing into their mouths: therefore you shall have night without vision, and you shall have darkness without divination; the sun shall go down on the prophets, and the day shall be dark for them. So the seers shall be ashamed, and the diviners abashed; indeed they shall all cover their lips; for *there is* no answer from God."

The Third Angel's Message / The Warning

Revelation 14:9–11

"Then a third angel followed them, saying with a loud voice, 'If anyone worships the beast and his image, and receives *his* mark on his forehead or on his hand, he himself shall also drink of the wine of the wrath of God, which is poured out full strength into the cup of His indignation. He shall be tormented with fire and brimstone in the presence of the holy angels and in the presence of the Lamb. And the smoke of their torment ascends forever and ever; and they have no rest day or night, who worship the beast and his image, and whoever receives the mark of his name.' "

The Great Controversy, p. 438

"In contrast to those who keep the commandments of God and have the faith of Jesus, the third angel points to another class, against whose errors a solemn and fearful warning is uttered: 'If any man worship the beast and his image, and receive his mark in his forehead, or in his hand, the same shall drink of the wine of the wrath of God.' Revelation 14:9, 10. A correct interpretation of the symbols employed is necessary to an understanding of this message. What is represented by the beast, the image, the mark?"

What is represented by the beast?

Revelation 12:9

"So the great dragon was cast out, that serpent of old, called the Devil and Satan, who deceives the whole world; he was cast to the earth, and his angels were cast out with him."

Revelation 13:1–10

"Then I stood on the sand of the sea. And I saw a beast rising up out of the sea, having seven heads and ten horns, and on his horns ten crowns, and on his heads a blasphemous name. Now the beast which I saw was like a leopard, his feet were like *the feet of* a bear, and his mouth like the mouth of a lion. The dragon gave him his power, his throne, and great authority. And I saw one of his heads as if it had been mortally wounded, and his deadly wound was healed. And all the world marveled and followed the beast. So they worshiped the dragon who gave authority to the beast; and they worshiped the beast, saying, 'Who *is* like the beast? Who is able to make war with him?'

"And he was given a mouth speaking great things and blasphemies, and he was given authority to continue for forty-two months. Then he opened his mouth in blasphemy against God, to blaspheme His name, His tabernacle, and those who dwell in heaven. It was granted to him to make war with the saints and to overcome them. And authority was given him over every tribe, tongue, and nation. All who dwell on the earth will worship him, whose names have not been written in the Book of Life of the Lamb slain from the foundation of the world.

"If anyone has an ear, let him hear. He who leads into captivity shall go into captivity; he who kills with the sword must be killed with the sword. Here is the patience and the faith of the saints."

The Great Controversy, pp. 438, 439

"The line of prophecy in which these symbols are found begins with Revelation 12, with the dragon that sought to destroy Christ at His birth. The dragon is said to be Satan (Revelation 12:9); he it was that moved upon Herod to put the Saviour to death. But the chief agent of Satan in making war upon Christ and His people during the first centuries of the Christian Era was the Roman Empire, in which paganism was the prevailing religion. Thus while the dragon, primarily, represents Satan, it is, in a secondary sense, a symbol of pagan Rome.

"In chapter 13 (verses 1–10) is described another beast, 'like unto a leopard,' to which the dragon gave 'his power, and his seat, and great authority.' This symbol, as most Protestants have believed, represents the papacy, which succeeded to the power and seat and authority once held by the ancient Roman empire. Of the leopardlike beast it is declared: 'There was given unto him a mouth speaking great things and blasphemies.... And he opened his mouth in blasphemy against God, to blaspheme His name, and His tabernacle, and them that dwell in heaven. And it was given unto him to make war with the saints, and to overcome them: and power was given him over all kindreds, and tongues, and nations.' This prophecy, which is nearly identical with the description of the little horn of Daniel 7, unquestionably points to the papacy."

What is represented by the image?

Revelation 13:11

"Then I saw another beast coming up out of the earth, and he had two horns like a lamb and spoke like a dragon."

Revelation 17:15

"Then he said to me, 'The waters which you saw, where the harlot sits, are peoples, multitudes, nations, and tongues.' "

The Great Controversy, p. 440

"But the beast with lamblike horns was seen 'coming up out of the earth [Revelation 13:11].' Instead of overthrowing other powers to establish itself, the nation thus represented must arise in territory previously unoccupied and grow up gradually and peacefully. It could not, then, arise among the crowded and struggling nationalities of the Old World—that turbulent sea of 'peoples, and multitudes, and nations, and tongues [Revelation 17:15].' It must be sought in the Western Continent.

"What nation of the New World was in 1798 rising into power, giving promise of strength and greatness, and attracting the attention of the world? The application of the symbol admits of no question. One nation, and only one, meets the specifications of this prophecy; it points unmistakably to the United States of America."

Revelation 13:16, 17

"He causes all, both small and great, rich and poor, free and slave, to receive a mark on their right hand or on their foreheads, and that no one may buy or sell except one who has the mark or the name of the beast, or the number of his name."

The Great Controversy, p. 445

"When the leading churches of the United States, uniting upon such points of doctrine as are held by them in common, shall influence the state to enforce their decrees and to sustain their institutions, then Protestant America will have formed an image of the Roman hierarchy, and the infliction of civil penalties upon dissenters will inevitably result.

"The beast with two horns 'causeth [commands] all, both small and great, rich and poor, free and bond, to receive a mark in their right hand, or in their foreheads: and that no man might buy or sell, save he that had the mark, or the name of the beast, or the number of his name.' Revelation 13:16, 17. The third angel's warning is: 'If any man worship the beast and his image, and receive his mark in his forehead, or in his hand, the same shall drink of the wine of the wrath of God [Revelation 14:9, 10].' 'The beast' mentioned in this message, whose worship is enforced by the two-horned beast, is the first, or leopardlike beast of Revelation 13—the papacy. The 'image to the beast' represents that form of apostate Protestantism which will be developed when the Protestant churches shall seek the aid of the civil power for the enforcement of their dogmas."

What is represented by the mark?

Daniel 7:25

"He shall speak *pompous* words against the Most High, shall persecute the saints of the Most High, and shall intend to change times and law. Then *the saints* shall be given into his hand for a time and times and half a time."

2 Thessalonians 2:3

"Let no one deceive you by any means; for *that Day will not come* unless the falling away comes first, and the man of sin is revealed, the son of perdition."

The Great Controversy, p. 446

"The special characteristic of the beast, and therefore of his image, is the breaking of God's commandments. Says Daniel, of the little horn, the papacy: 'He shall think to change times and the law.' Daniel 7:25, R.V. And Paul styled the same power the 'man of sin [2 Thessalonians 2:3],' who was to exalt himself above God. One prophecy is a complement of the other. Only by changing God's law could the papacy exalt itself above God;

whoever should understandingly keep the law as thus changed would be giving supreme honor to that power by which the change was made. Such an act of obedience to papal laws would be a mark of allegiance to the pope in the place of God.

"The papacy has attempted to change the law of God. The second commandment, forbidding image worship, has been dropped from the law, and the fourth commandment has been so changed as to authorize the observance of the first instead of the seventh day as the Sabbath. But papists urge, as a reason for omitting the second commandment, that it is unnecessary, being included in the first, and that they are giving the law exactly as God designed it to be understood. This cannot be the change foretold by the prophet. An intentional, deliberate change is presented: 'He shall *think* to change the times and the law [Daniel 7:25].' The change in the fourth commandment exactly fulfills the prophecy. For this the only authority claimed is that of the church. Here the papal power openly sets itself above God."

The Great Controversy, pp. 449, 450

"But when Sunday observance shall be enforced by law, and the world shall be enlightened concerning the obligation of the true Sabbath, then whoever shall transgress the command of God, to obey a precept which has no higher authority than that of Rome, will thereby honor popery above God. He is paying homage to Rome and to the power which enforces the institution ordained by Rome. He is worshiping the beast and his image. As men then reject the institution which God has declared to be the sign of His authority, and honor in its stead that which Rome has chosen as the token of her supremacy, they will thereby accept the sign of allegiance to Rome—'the mark of the beast.' And it is not until the issue is thus plainly set before the people, and they are brought to choose between the commandments of God and the commandments of men, that those who continue in transgression will receive 'the mark of the beast.'

"The most fearful threatening ever addressed to mortals is contained in the third angel's message. That must be a terrible sin which calls down the wrath of God unmingled with mercy. Men are not to be left in darkness concerning this important matter; the warning against this sin is to be given to the world before the visitation of God's judgments, that all may know why they are to be inflicted, and have opportunity to escape them. Prophecy declares that the first angel would make his announcement to 'every nation, and kindred, and tongue, and people [Revelation 14:6].' The warning of the third angel, which forms a part of the same threefold message, is to be no less widespread. It is represented in the prophecy as being proclaimed with a loud voice, by an angel flying in the midst of heaven; and it will command the attention of the world."

> "The mark of the beast is the papal sabbath, which has been accepted by the world in the place of the day of God's appointment."

The Signs of the Times, November 8, 1899

"The change of the Sabbath is a sign or mark of the authority of the Romish Church. Those who, understanding the claims of the fourth commandment, choose to observe the false sabbath in the place of the true, are thereby paying homage to that power by which alone it is commanded. The mark of the beast is the papal sabbath, which has been accepted by the world in the place of the day of God's appointment."

The Third Angel's Message / The Solution

Revelation 14:12

"Here is the patience of the saints; here *are* those who keep the commandments of God and the faith of Jesus."

Selected Messages, Book 3, p. 172

"The third angel's message is the proclamation of the commandments of God and the faith of Jesus Christ. The commandments of God have been proclaimed, but the faith of Jesus Christ has not been proclaimed by Seventh-day Adventists as of equal importance, the law and the gospel going hand in hand. I cannot find language to express this subject in its fullness.

" 'The faith of Jesus.' It is talked of, but not understood. What constitutes the faith of Jesus, that belongs to the third angel's message? Jesus becoming our sin-bearer that He might become our sin-pardoning Saviour. He was treated as we deserve to be treated. He came to our world and took our sins that we might take His righteousness. And faith in the ability of Christ to save us amply and fully and entirely is the faith of Jesus."

Revelation 11:19

"Then the temple of God was opened in heaven, and the ark of His covenant was seen in His temple. And there were lightnings, noises, thunderings, an earthquake, and great hail."

Revelation 12:17

"And the dragon was enraged with the woman, and he went to make war with the rest of her offspring, who keep the commandments of God and have the testimony of Jesus Christ."

Revelation 19:10

"And I fell at his feet to worship him. But he said to me, 'See *that you do* not *do that*! I am your fellow servant, and of your brethren who have the testimony of Jesus. Worship God! For the testimony of Jesus is the spirit of prophecy.' "

Early Writings, p. 254

"As the ministration of Jesus closed in the holy place, and He passed into the holiest, and stood before the ark containing the law of God, He sent another mighty angel with a third message to the world. A parchment was placed in the angel's hand, and as he descended to the earth in power and majesty, he proclaimed a fearful warning, with the most terrible threatening ever borne to man. This message was designed to put the children of God upon their guard, by showing them the hour of temptation and anguish that was before them. Said the angel, 'They will be brought into close combat with the beast and his image. Their only hope of eternal life is to remain steadfast. Although their lives are at stake, they must hold fast the truth.' The third angel closes his message thus: 'Here is the patience of the saints: here are they that keep the commandments of God, and the faith of Jesus [Revelation 14:12].' As he repeated these words, he pointed to the heavenly sanctuary. The minds of all who embrace this message are directed to the most holy place, where Jesus stands before the ark, making His final intercession for all those for whom mercy still lingers and for those who have ignorantly broken the law of God."

Early Writings, pp. 254, 255
"After Jesus opened the door of the most holy, the light of the Sabbath was seen, and the people of God were tested, as the children of Israel were tested anciently, to see if they would keep God's law. I saw the third angel pointing upward, showing the disappointed ones the way to the holiest of the heavenly sanctuary. As they by faith enter the most holy, they find Jesus, and hope and joy spring up anew. I saw them looking back, reviewing the past, from the proclamation of the second advent of Jesus, down through their experience to the passing of the time in 1844. They see their disappointment explained, and joy and certainty again animate them. The third angel has lighted up the past, the present, and the future, and they know that God has indeed led them by His mysterious providence.

"It was represented to me that the remnant followed Jesus into the most holy place and beheld the ark and the mercy seat, and were captivated with their glory."

> *"The third angel has lighted up the past, the present, and the future, and they know that God has indeed led them by His mysterious providence."*

Early Writings, p. 256
"Many who embraced the third message had not had an experience in the two former messages. Satan understood this, and his evil eye was upon them to overthrow them; but the third angel was pointing them to the most holy place, and those who had had an experience in the past messages were pointing them the way to the heavenly sanctuary. Many saw the perfect chain of truth in the angels' messages, and gladly received them in their order, and followed Jesus by faith into the heavenly sanctuary. These messages were represented to me as an anchor to the people of God. Those who understand and receive them will be kept from being swept away by the many delusions of Satan."

> *"The true understanding of these messages is of vital importance. The destiny of souls hangs upon the manner in which they are received."*

Early Writings, pp. 258, 259
"I saw a company who stood well guarded and firm, giving no countenance to those who would unsettle the established faith of the body. God looked upon them with approbation. I was shown three steps—the first, second, and third angels' messages. Said my accompanying angel, 'Woe to him who shall move a block or stir a pin of these messages. The true understanding of these messages is of vital importance. The destiny of souls hangs upon the manner in which they are received.' I was again brought down through these messages, and saw how dearly the people of God had purchased their experience. It had been obtained through much suffering and severe conflict. God had led them along step by step, until He had placed them upon a solid, immovable platform."

Early Writings, p. 259

"Satan led on those who rejected the message of John [the Baptist] to go still farther, to reject and crucify Christ. In doing this they placed themselves where they could not receive the blessing on the day of Pentecost, which would have taught them the way into the heavenly sanctuary."

Early Writings, p. 260

"The great Sacrifice had been offered and had been accepted, and the Holy Spirit which descended on the day of Pentecost carried the minds of the disciples from the earthly sanctuary to the heavenly, where Jesus had entered by His own blood, to shed upon His disciples the benefits of His atonement. But the Jews were left in total darkness. They lost all the light which they might have had upon the plan of salvation, and still trusted in their useless sacrifices and offerings. The heavenly sanctuary had taken the place of the earthly, yet they had no knowledge of the change. Therefore they could not be benefited by the mediation of Christ in the holy place."

Early Writings, pp. 260, 261

"Those who rejected the first [angel's] message could not be benefited by the second; neither were they benefited by the midnight cry, which was to prepare them to enter with Jesus by faith into the most holy place of the heavenly sanctuary. And by rejecting the two former messages, they have so darkened their understanding that they can see no light in the third angel's message, which shows the way into the most holy place. I saw that as the Jews crucified Jesus, so the nominal churches had crucified these messages, and therefore they have no knowledge of the way into the most holy, and they cannot be benefited by the intercession of Jesus there. Like the Jews, who offered

their useless sacrifices, they offer up their useless prayers to the apartment which Jesus has left; and Satan, pleased with the deception, assumes a religious character, and leads the minds of these professed Christians to himself, working with his power, his signs and lying wonders, to fasten them in his snare."

Early Writings, p. 261

"Satan deceives some with Spiritualism. He also comes as an angel of light [2 Corinthians 11:14] and spreads his influence over the land by means of false reformations. The churches are elated, and consider that God is working marvelously for them, when it is the work of another spirit. The excitement will die away and leave the world and the church in a worse condition than before.

"I saw that God has honest children among the nominal Adventists and the fallen churches, and before the plagues shall be poured out, ministers and people will be called out from these churches and will gladly receive the truth. Satan knows this; and before the loud cry of the third angel is given, he raises an excitement in these religious bodies, that those who have rejected the truth may think that God is with them. He hopes to deceive the honest and lead them to think that God is still working for the churches."

The Great Controversy, p. 613

"When the third angel's message closes, mercy no longer pleads for the guilty inhabitants of the earth."

The Great Controversy, p. 594

"The death of Jesus as fully destroyed their [the disciples'] hopes as if He had not forewarned them. So in the prophecies the future is opened before us as plainly as it was opened to the disciples by the words of Christ. The events connected with the close of probation and the work of preparation for the time of trouble, are clearly presented. But multitudes have no more understanding of these important truths than if they had never been revealed. Satan watches to catch away every impression that would make them wise unto salvation, and the time of trouble will find them unready.

"When God sends to men warnings so important that they are represented as proclaimed by holy angels flying in the midst of heaven, He requires every person endowed with reasoning powers to heed the message. The fearful judgments denounced against the worship of the beast and his image (Revelation 14:9–11), should lead all to a diligent study of the prophecies to learn what the mark of the beast is, and how they are to avoid receiving it."

The Loud Cry of the Third Angel

Revelation 18:1–4

"After these things I saw another angel coming down from heaven, having great authority, and the earth was illuminated with his glory. And he cried mightily with a loud voice, saying, 'Babylon the great is fallen, is fallen, and has become a dwelling place of demons, a prison for every foul spirit, and a cage for every unclean and hated bird! For all the nations have drunk of the wine of the wrath of her fornication, the kings of the earth have committed fornication with her, and the merchants of the earth have become rich through the abundance of her luxury.'

"And I heard another voice from heaven saying, 'Come out of her, my people, lest you share in her sins, and lest you receive of her plagues.' "

The Great Controversy, p. 603

" 'I saw another angel come down from heaven, having great power; and the earth was lightened with his glory. And he cried mightily with a strong voice, saying, Babylon the great is fallen, is fallen, and is become the habitation of devils, and the hold of every foul spirit, and a cage of every unclean and hateful bird.' 'And I heard another voice from heaven, saying, Come out of her, My people, that ye be not partakers of her sins, and that ye receive not of her plagues.' Revelation 18:1, 2, 4.

"This scripture points forward to a time when the announcement of the fall of Babylon, as made by the second angel of Revelation 14 (verse 8), is to be repeated, with the additional mention of the corruptions which have been entering the various organizations that constitute Babylon, since that message was first given, in the summer of 1844."

The Great Controversy, p. 604

"God still has a people in Babylon; and before the visitation of His judgments these faithful ones must be called out, that they partake not of her sins and 'receive not of her plagues [Revelation 18:4].' Hence the movement symbolized by the angel coming down from heaven, lightening the earth with his glory and crying mightily with a strong voice, announcing the sins of Babylon. In connection with his message the call is heard: 'Come out of her, My people [Revelation 18:4].' These announcements, uniting with the third angel's message, constitute the final warning to be given to the inhabitants of the earth."

The Great Controversy, 605

"The Sabbath will be the great test of loyalty, for it is the point of truth especially controverted. When the final test shall be brought to bear upon men, then the line of distinction will be drawn between those who serve God and those who serve Him not. While the observance of the false sabbath in compliance with the law of the state, contrary to the fourth commandment, will be an avowal of allegiance to a power that is in opposition to God, the keeping of the true Sabbath, in obedience to God's law, is an evidence of loyalty to the Creator. While one class, by accepting the sign of submission to earthly powers, receive the mark of the beast, the other choosing the token of allegiance to divine authority, receive the seal of God."

2 Thessalonians 2:10–12

"And with all unrighteous deception among those who perish, because they did not receive the love of the truth, that they might be saved. And for this reason God will send them strong delusion, that they should believe the lie, that they all may be condemned who did not believe the truth but had pleasure in unrighteousness."

The Review and Herald, December 18, 1888

"Satan came as an angel of light in the wilderness of temptation to deceive Christ; and he does not come to man in a hideous form, as he is sometimes represented, but as an angel of light. He will come personating Jesus Christ, working mighty miracles; and men will fall down and worship him as Jesus Christ. We shall be commanded to worship this being, whom the world will glorify as Christ. What shall we do?—Tell them that Christ has warned us against just such a foe, who is man's worst enemy, yet who claims to be God; and that when Christ shall make his appearance, it will be with power and great glory, accompanied by ten thousand times ten thousand angels and thousands of thousands; and that when he shall come, we shall know his voice."

Revelation 1:13–15

"And in the midst of the seven lampstands *One* like the Son of Man, clothed with a garment down to the feet and girded about the chest with a golden band. His head and hair *were* white like wool, as white as snow, and His eyes like a flame of fire; His feet *were* like fine brass, as if refined in a furnace, and His voice as the sound of many waters."

> *"One class, by accepting the sign of submission to earthly powers, receive the mark of the beast, the other choosing the token of allegiance to divine authority, receive the seal of God."*

The Great Controversy, p. 624

"As the crowning act in the great drama of deception, Satan himself will personate Christ. The church has long professed to look to the Saviour's advent as the consummation of her hopes. Now the great deceiver will make it appear that Christ has come. In different parts of the earth, Satan will manifest himself among men as a majestic being of dazzling brightness, resembling the description of the Son of God given by John in the Revelation. Revelation 1:13–15. The glory that surrounds him is unsurpassed by anything that mortal eyes have yet beheld. The shout of triumph rings out upon the air: 'Christ has come! Christ has come!' The people prostrate themselves in adoration before him, while he lifts up his hands and pronounces a blessing upon them, as Christ blessed His disciples when He was upon the earth. His voice is soft and subdued, yet full of melody. In gentle, compassionate tones he presents some of the same gracious, heavenly truths which the Saviour uttered; he heals the diseases of the people, and then, in his assumed character of Christ, he claims to have changed the Sabbath to Sunday, and commands all to hallow the day which he has blessed. He declares that those who persist in keeping holy the seventh day are blaspheming his name by refusing to listen to his angels sent to them with light and truth. This is the strong, almost overmastering delusion."

The Great Controversy, p. 390

"Revelation 18 points to the time when, as the result of rejecting the threefold warning of Revelation 14:6–12, the church will have fully reached the condition foretold by the second angel, and the people of God still in Babylon will be called upon to separate from her communion. This message is the last that will ever be given to the world; and it will accomplish its work. When those that 'believed not the truth, but had pleasure in unrighteousness' (2 Thessalonians 2:12), shall be left to receive strong delusion and to believe a lie, then the light of truth will shine upon all whose hearts are open to receive it, and all the children of the Lord that remain in Babylon will heed the call: 'Come out of her, My people' (Revelation 18:4)."

Hosea 6:3

"Let us know, let us pursue the knowledge of the Lord. His going forth is established as the morning; He will come to us like the rain, like the latter *and* former rain to the earth."

The Great Controversy, p. 611

"The angel who unites in the proclamation of the third angel's message is to lighten the whole earth with his glory. A work of worldwide extent and unwonted power is here

foretold. The advent movement of 1840–44 was a glorious manifestation of the power of God; the first angel's message was carried to every missionary station in the world, and in some countries there was the greatest religious interest which has been witnessed in any land since the Reformation of the sixteenth century; but these are to be exceeded by the mighty movement under the last warning of the third angel.

"The work will be similar to that of the Day of Pentecost. As the 'former rain' was given, in the outpouring of the Holy Spirit at the opening of the gospel, to cause the upspringing of the precious seed, so the 'latter rain' will be given at its close for the ripening of the harvest. 'Then shall we know, if we follow on to know the Lord: His going forth is prepared as the morning; and He shall come unto us as the rain, as the latter and former rain unto the earth.' Hosea 6:3."

Early Writings, pp. 277–279

"I saw angels hurrying to and fro in heaven, descending to the earth, and again ascending to heaven, preparing for the fulfillment of some important event. Then I saw another mighty angel commissioned to descend to the earth, to unite his voice with the third angel, and give power and force to his message. Great power and glory were imparted to the angel, and as he descended, the earth was lightened with his glory. The light which attended this angel penetrated everywhere, as he cried mightily, with a strong voice, 'Babylon the great is fallen, is fallen, and is become the habitation of devils, and the hold of every foul spirit, and a cage of every unclean and hateful bird [Revelation 18:2].' The message of the fall of Babylon, as given by the second angel, is repeated, with the additional mention of the corruptions which have been entering the churches since

1844. The work of this angel comes in at the right time to join in the last great work of the third angel's message as it swells to a loud cry. And the people of God are thus prepared to stand in the hour of temptation, which they are soon to meet. I saw a great light resting upon them, and they united to fearlessly proclaim the third angel's message.

"Angels were sent to aid the mighty angel from heaven, and I heard voices which seemed to sound everywhere, 'Come out of her, My people, that ye be not partakers of her sins, and that ye receive not of her plagues. For her sins have reached unto heaven, and God hath remembered her iniquities [Revelation 18:4].' This message seemed to be an addition to the third message, joining it as the midnight cry joined the second angel's message in 1844. The glory of God rested upon the patient, waiting saints, and they fearlessly gave the last solemn warning, proclaiming the fall of Babylon and calling upon God's people to come out of her that they might escape her fearful doom.

"The light that was shed upon the waiting ones penetrated everywhere, and those in the churches who had any light, who had not heard and rejected the three messages, obeyed the call and left the fallen churches. Many had come to years of accountability since these messages had been given, and the light shone upon them, and they were privileged to choose life or death. Some chose life and took their stand with those who were looking for their Lord and keeping all His commandments. The third message was to do its work; all were to be tested upon it, and the precious ones were to be called out from the religious bodies. A compelling power moved the honest, while the manifestation of the power of God brought a fear and restraint upon their unbelieving relatives and friends so that they dared not, neither had they the power to, hinder those who felt the work of the Spirit of God upon them. The last call was carried even to the poor slaves, and the pious among them poured forth their songs of rapturous joy at the prospect of their happy deliverance. Their masters could not check them; fear and astonishment kept them silent. Mighty miracles were wrought, the sick were healed, and signs and wonders followed the believers. God was in the work, and every saint, fearless of consequences, followed the convictions of his own conscience and united with those who were keeping all the commandments of God; and with power they sounded abroad the third message. I saw that this message will close with power and strength far exceeding the midnight cry.

"Servants of God, endowed with power from on high with their faces lighted up, and shining with holy consecration, went forth to proclaim the message from heaven. Souls that were scattered all through the religious bodies answered to the call, and the precious were hurried out of the doomed churches, as Lot was hurried out of Sodom before her destruction. God's people were strengthened by the excellent glory which rested upon them in rich abundance and prepared them to endure the hour of temptation. I heard everywhere a multitude of voices saying, 'Here is the patience of the saints: here are they that keep the commandments of God, and the faith of Jesus' [Revelation 14:12]. "

Contact Information

If you desire a deeper study into these truths, please contact Revelation Ministry at www.1ref.us/revelationmin

Bibliography

White, Ellen G. *The Acts of the Apostles.* Mountain View, CA: Pacific Press Publishing Association, 1911.

———. "After the Crucifixion." *The Youth's Instructor*, April 25, 1901.

———. *Counsels on Sabbath School Work.* Washington, DC: Review and Herald Publishing Association, 1938.

———. *Counsels to Writers and Editors.* Nashville, TN: Southern Publishing Association, 1946.

———. "David's Prayer." *The Review and Herald*, December 18, 1888.

———. *The Desire of Ages.* Mountain View, CA: Pacific Press Publishing Association, 1898.

———. *Early Writings.* Washington, DC: Review and Herald Publishing Association, 1882.

———. *Education.* Mountain View, CA: Pacific Press Publishing Association, 1903.

———. *Evangelism.* Washington, DC: Review and Herald Publishing Association, 1946.

———. *The Great Controversy.* Mountain View, CA: Pacific Press Publishing Association, 1911.

———. Manuscript 14, 1901.

———. *Manuscript Releases.* Vol. 1. Silver Spring, MD: Ellen G. White Estate, 1981.

———. *Manuscript Releases.* Vol. 12. Silver Spring, MD: Ellen G. White Estate, 1990.

———. "Obedience the Condition of Salvation." *The Signs of the Times*, November 30, 1904.

———. *Patriarchs and Prophets.* Washington, DC: Review and Herald Publishing Association, 1890.

———. "The Relation of Christ to the Law Is Not Understood." *The Review and Herald*, February 4, 1890.

———. "The Seal of God—No. 2." *The Signs of the Times*, November 8, 1899.

———. *Selected Messages.* Book 2. Washington, DC: Review and Herald Publishing Association, 1958.

———. *Selected Messages.* Book 3. Washington, DC: Review and Herald Publishing Association, 1980.

———. *Steps to Christ.* Mountain View, CA: Pacific Press Publishing Association, 1892.

———. *The Story of Redemption.* Hagerstown, MD: Review and Herald Publishing Association, 1947.

———. *Testimonies for the Church.* Vol. 6. Mountain View, CA: Pacific Press Publishing Association, 1901.

We invite you to view the complete
selection of titles we publish at:

www.TEACHServices.com

Scan with your mobile
device to go directly
to our website.

Please write or email us your praises, reactions, or
thoughts about this or any other book we publish at:

P.O. Box 954
Ringgold, GA 30736

info@TEACHServices.com

TEACH Services, Inc., titles may be purchased in bulk for
educational, business, fund-raising, or sales promotional use.
For information, please e-mail:

BulkSales@TEACHServices.com

Finally, if you are interested in seeing
your own book in print, please contact us at

publishing@TEACHServices.com

We would be happy to review your manuscript for free.

CPSIA information can be obtained at www.ICGtesting.com
Printed in the USA
LVOW02s2030010915

451921LV00005B/2/P

9 781479 605057